HOME COOKING
FOR YOUR DOG

HOME COOKING
— FOR YOUR DOG —

75 HOLISTIC RECIPES
FOR A HEALTHIER DOG

CHRISTINE M. FILARDI

WITH DR. WAYNE GELTMAN, DVM

ILLUSTRATIONS BY MICHAEL WELDON

STEWART, TABORI & CHANG   NEW YORK

CONTENTS

1 A HEALTHY DOG DIET · 13

FOREWORD

I am a veterinarian who has, over time, evolved a more natural and holistic approach to medicine. Since graduating from veterinary school in 1994, I have pursued various opportunities to incorporate alternative healing modalities into my practice because I have seen the amazing health benefits they offer.

Recently, the demand for natural products and alternative services for pets has increased dramatically and the marketplace has responded accordingly. As people are experiencing the benefits of a more holistic approach to their own healthcare, many are seeking the same for their pets.

The term "holistic veterinary care" is actually a very simple concept. It means looking at the whole patient, which includes the medical history, diet, environment, potential toxin exposure, stress factors, and the animal's relationship with its owner. A treatment protocol is developed, integrating the best traditional and alternative options. In my view, this integrative approach is the way all medicine should be practiced. (In most acute situations—for example, severe trauma or certain types of infections—however, the best treatment will involve modern surgical techniques and drug therapy from conventional Western medicine.)

Many alternative therapies offer preventive benefits in healthy pets, can be used as an adjunct in acute conditions, and—most important—can be used to determine and treat the "root" problem in many chronic conditions. I utilize a wide variety of holistic treatments in my practice, such as acupuncture, low-level laser therapy, and herbal and homeopathic remedies. The common principle of all these treatments is to restore balance and homeostasis in the patient to promote healing. These techniques are used to treat a wide variety of conditions including arthritis, disc disease, allergies, anxiety, and chronic pain.

The cornerstone of a holistic approach to healthcare is proper nutrition. Just like us, our pets truly are what they eat, and I believe in feeding a species-appropriate diet. The highly processed kibble and canned foods we have fed our pets for decades are not the best we can offer them. I advocate all-natural foods that are the least processed and most species appropriate and recommend both raw and home-cooked diets that are complete and balanced. Periodically changing the protein source and limiting or removing grain will decrease the risk of the pet developing allergies.

When I counsel a new puppy or kitten owner, the first thing I discuss is diet, because it is that important. I tell owners that feeding a complete and balanced raw or home-cooked diet that has the proper ratio of quality ingredients and supplements is the best they can do for their pet. In my practice, I have personally seen dramatic improvements in the health of patients with diet change alone. Getting pets off of highly processed dry food and onto natural whole foods that include meats, vegetables, limited grains, and appropriate supplements is the first step. I have seen myriad problems, such as obesity, allergies, skin problems, and gastrointestinal issues, improve dramatically or resolve completely by simply changing to an appropriate raw or home-cooked diet.

I believe what is espoused in human medicine should be the same principles we follow with our pets: Eat a healthy, balanced diet; drink pure water; avoid toxin exposure whenever possible; exercise; maintain an appropriate weight; and get plenty of rest (which most of our pets never seem to have a problem doing!). This book is a great tool to help your dog get started on the journey toward healthier living.

Dr. Wayne Geltman, DVM
ALL CREATURES VETERINARY SERVICES
LONG BEACH, NEW YORK

INTRODUCTION

I've learned it's the small, seemingly unremarkable events that have the most impact on our lives. This is especially true of my journey to becoming a holistic chef for animals. As a dog owner and an animal lover, there have been countless little moments and experiences with my dogs that have made me stop and reevaluate my approach to their care. I constantly ask myself, what can I do to make their lives better? Am I really doing everything I can to ensure they are leading happy, healthy lives?

One such event occurred several years ago, when I was watching my shepherd mix, Madeline, play with a marrow bone on the living room rug. Marrow bones are one of my favorite things to give my dogs as treats because they're excellent for their teeth and they keep the dogs busy for a good hour or two. Countless days I watched my dogs enjoying these bones on the living room rug, until one day I noticed something I had never really considered before. Madeline spent a lot of time with her marrow bone. She would toss it in the air, drop it on the rug, and pick it up over and over again. As I watched her, I wondered what the wet bone was picking up from the rug and transporting into her body. At that point, Madeline had been suffering from chronic upset stomach and digestion issues. I found myself steam-cleaning the rugs weekly because she was constantly getting sick on them. Then it occurred to me: Was she constantly getting sick because I was constantly steam-cleaning the rugs?

It became obvious to me, as I watched Madeline with her marrow bone on the living room rug that day, that the products I was using to clean the rugs—and quite frankly my whole apartment—were probably causing her upset stomach. I eventually removed all of my rugs. One day, several weeks later, I passed the steam cleaner collecting dust in the basement. At that moment I realized that since removing the rugs, Madeline hadn't gotten sick once. It was from this experience that I began to question how my living environment was affecting the health of my pets.

Then, in 2005, I met Boo. I was volunteering with Animal Control of Westchester County, New York, when I walked past a dog that had recently come into the shelter. His name was Boo, and he was not in good shape. He had lost nearly half of his fur, exposing reddish-pink, raw, inflamed skin. He was itching incessantly. I was completely overwhelmed by the sight of him. I went straight to the office to inquire about his condition but no one seemed to know what was wrong with him or how else to help him. This answer felt instinctively wrong and confusing to me.

I decided at that moment I would take Boo home as a foster dog. On June 6, 2005, I walked out of the shelter with Boo and a box of numerous medications I was told he would be on for the rest of his life.

The first thing I did when I got home was throw out the box of medications. I was convinced that I could nurse him back to health without any medicine at all. It took me nine months to completely transform his health on a regimen of supplements and home-cooked and raw dog food. All his hair grew back, he no longer suffered from inflamed and itchy skin, and his coat began to shine. He was with me for five years before he passed away in July 2010, and I hope they were the best years of his life.

But the moment that had the most significant impact on my journey to becoming a holistic chef for animals actually happened nearly a decade ago. I was walking my dogs on the beach one summer morning when I met a woman named J.R. She was walking her own dogs, and as our dogs played together, we started talking. Seemingly out of nowhere she asked, "What are you feeding your dogs?" I had never really considered this before. "Dog food?" I replied. In a few sentences she explained the terribly poor quality of most commercial pet food and the serious health issues consuming it can cause. She suggested I try the BARF, or Bones and Raw Food, diet. I required no convincing that this approach made sense.

I gradually transitioned my dogs onto the BARF diet. Day after day, I realized how much happier they were at feeding time, how much shinier their coats became, how they rarely stopped to scratch anymore, and how they no longer suffered from bouts of upset stomach.

On thinking about it, you can begin to see how all of these events represent different and very important aspects of a dog's life that significantly affect its health: what it eats, its medical issues and how those issues are treated, and the environment in which it lives. My vision for this book is to help dog owners create and maintain a state of optimal health for their companion animals. They rely on us to make the right decisions for them, to keep them safe, happy, and healthy, and we owe it to them to give them the best life possible.

Finally, I express my absolute gratitude for meeting J.R. that morning on the beach. One single question led me in the direction of my true calling, my absolute passion, and my greatest love. *Thank You* will never be enough.

THE ANIMAL RESCUE INITIATIVE

Back in January 2012, I met Jackie—my editor at Stewart, Tabori & Chang—at a dog adoption event in New York. I was working the morning shift at the event and was responsible for handling a dog named Chowder, a beautiful boxer mix who was looking for his forever home. Jackie was scheduled to handle Chowder for the afternoon. As we switched shifts, we chatted for a bit about my profession as a holistic chef for animals. We exchanged information, and I gave her a few of my recipes to try for her own dog. A few weeks later, she called me to ask me if I'd be interested in writing a cookbook for dogs, and the rest is history.

If it weren't for that adoption event, and for Chowder in particular, I might never have met Jackie and this book might have never happened. As part of the local animal rescue community and an active member of the ASPCA, I see so many deserving animals in need of loving homes. It seems only natural that I give back to animals like Chowder by starting an animal rescue initiative of my own and donating part of my proceeds to animal rescue. So far, we have helped several dogs, such as Brutus, who was rescued in March 2013 from a home where he was kept outside on a chain. After getting medical attention and treating heartworm, Brutus began training and is on his way to finding the loving home he deserves. You can visit my website at www.bowmeowraw.com to see updates on these dogs and read stories of other animals we've helped through this initiative.

If you are considering adding a furry friend to your family, I strongly encourage you to go to your local shelter and adopt. There are so many wonderful animals in need of loving homes. With multiple rescues of my own, I know how rewarding adopting a pet can be and the joy they bring to my life every day.

CHAPTER 1

A HEALTHY DOG DIET

AS DOG OWNERS, WE ARE RESPONSIBLE FOR THE HEALTH AND WELL-BEING OF OUR FURRY FRIENDS and a significant part of their well-being is dictated by what they eat. Just like us, our dogs want to eat healthy and nutritious food that actually tastes good! As the old adage goes, "You Are What You Eat," and this applies to our dogs as well.

A healthy dog diet, much like a healthy human diet, is free of toxins, pesticides, carcinogens, fillers, and processed foods. Unfortunately, much of the commercial pet food on the market today is loaded with harmful ingredients that can compromise your dog's health. As more and more people have realized this, the concept of cooking homemade dog food has become increasingly popular.

Although cooking homemade food for your dog may seem like an overwhelming undertaking and a stark transition from simply scooping a cup of dry dog food into your dog's bowl, it's well worth it. If your dog has suffered from allergies, itchy skin, and any other health problems, a homemade diet can do absolute wonders—not only physically, but emotionally and behaviorally as well. I've seen dogs go from crabby couch potatoes who turned up their noses at every meal to happy, excited, energetic, and playful dogs who eagerly anticipate dinnertime after just a few weeks on a homemade diet. Equally important is that you are satisfying one of their most basic needs—the need for proper nourishment.

This chapter is meant to help you understand the basics of cooking for your dog. If I could convince you of one thing, it would be that you don't have to approach it as all or nothing. If you begin small, perhaps just making one or two meals a week, you will hopefully realize that cooking for your dog is easy, fun, and very rewarding.

THE PROBLEM WITH COMMERCIAL PET FOOD

You may be asking yourself, "Why switch now when commercial dog food has been around for quite a while?" It's been around for a while, but not forever. There are a whole host of problems with commercial pet food, but let's start with one of the most significant: It is not nutritionally comparable to what a dog would eat in the wild. Dogs are natural predators and carnivores and, before they were domesticated, they had to hunt and kill prey to eat and survive. Even though dogs have been domesticated for thousands of years, they are still biologically engineered to consume a diet that mimics what they might find in the wild—things like turkey, chicken, and duck. Not only do wild dogs consume wild game, but they also consume the nutrient-rich organs of these animals, like the stomach, heart, and liver.

Commercial pet food wasn't developed until about 100 years ago. We've essentially forced the modern dog to eat, somewhat for our own convenience, what *we* as humans think they should eat, without having much consideration for their nutritional needs and their biological makeup. Many commercial foods don't include essential ingredients like organ meat, and instead bulk up the kibble with things like grain and animal by-products, which can be almost any part of an animal. As terrible as it sounds, many commercial pet foods include by-products like hair, tissue, feathers, and other animal parts deemed nonconsumable for humans. Including by-products like these allows pet food companies to bulk up the food while keeping it very cheap. Many commercial dog foods are also sprayed with added fat to make the kibble more palatable for our pets. Is it any wonder our dogs are now overweight, and could it be partly the result of this added fat (of which most pet owners aren't even aware)?

Another issue with commercial pet food is that it's not strictly regulated by the FDA, which leads to questionable standards and even more questionable ingredients. Many commercial pet foods are loaded with additives and unlisted preservatives that extend shelf life and keep fat from going rancid. Common preservatives include BHA, BHT, and ethoxyquin. All of these can cause serious health issues in our pets. Unhealthy additives like food coloring, sweeteners, texturizers, and fats are often used to make the food more appealing to dogs and enhance taste and appearance. By law, however, not all preservatives have to be listed on the label, such as the ones added by companies supplying the raw ingredients to the food manufacturers.

HOW TO READ A DOG FOOD LABEL

Although there are many commercial dog foods that are extremely unhealthy for your dog, there are some holistic and organic dog foods that have come on the market in the past few years that offer better, healthier options. No matter what kind of dog food you choose to feed your dog, it's very important to understand what a dog food label is telling you about what exactly is in the food. Given the lack of regulation in the pet food industry, this can be hard, since pet food companies are not required to be nearly as transparent with the ingredients as they should be.

Many of the fillers and by-products included in commercial pet food come from rendering plants, which process these "ingredients" and then sell them to pet food companies. The dirty little secret of the pet food industry is that a significant amount of the by-products come from animals that are categorized as dead, dying, diseased, or disabled at slaughter.

Slaughterhouses will sell what they can't sell for human consumption to pet food companies to use in pet food, and the pet food companies label this as simply "by-product."

Given this, if the first or second ingredient in a dog food is "animal by-product," that's a red flag. In some of the healthier dog foods, ingredients like deboned chicken, vegetables, and brown rice are often the first ingredients listed.

A HOLISTIC DOG LIFESTYLE

Even though there are some healthier commercial dog foods available, the only way to really be sure that your dog is getting a good healthy meal is to cook for her. If you like to cook already, like I do, you'll find that it's easy and rewarding to cook for your dog. Besides knowing that my dogs are getting good, hearty, nutritious meals that are free of preservatives and toxins, cooking for them allows me to take a holistic approach to their wellness.

A "holistic" approach to pet care considers the different aspects of a dog's life that create the "whole" of their daily living. It aims to create the healthiest environment possible from the inside to the outside. This means that all aspects of a dog's life are considered. We can feed our pet a high-quality diet, but are we also providing a safe living environment free from toxins? Are we providing a toxin-free environment but feeding poor-quality treats with questionable ingredients? Are we giving our dogs enough exercise and quality time with us?

I strongly believe a holistic approach is the best approach. All of my recipes are written with the whole pet in mind. There is great variety in all of my recipes, as I am always using different vegetables, animal proteins, and grains. Variety is extremely important—just as it is in human diets—because we want to provide our dogs with all the vitamins and minerals needed for health and vitality.

A HOLISTIC APPROACH TO EXERCISE

Mental and physical exercise is an important aspect of holistic care. "It is not enough to simply take your dog to the dog park," explains dog trainer Julio Rivera. "Your dog needs structured walks, should be taught obedience commands, taken for hikes along trails, and have interactive play with you. This helps create a balanced and ultimately happy dog," he adds. Julio has helped me implement this multifaceted approach with my own rescues. It's very beneficial, especially for dogs with behavior challenges, to address issues in all areas of the dog's life. With a balanced homemade diet, mental and physical exercise, training, and obedience, my dogs have made tremendous progress.

In addition to a homemade diet, a holistic approach to dog care should include things like:

- Using green cleaning products in your home
- Providing safe toys for your dog to play with
- Giving your dog regular mental and physical exercise

HOLISTIC VETS

I find that taking my dogs to a veterinarian who understands some of my holistic approaches makes it much easier for me to maintain my dogs' holistic lifestyle. In addition to the growing number of holistic vets nationwide, many traditional vets are beginning to incorporate holistic approaches into their practices. I find that it's important to use a vet who understands the significant role of nutrition and its tremendous effect on the overall well-being of a dog, and who supports feeding a homemade diet.

To find a holistic vet near you, you can visit the American Holistic Veterinary Medical Association at www.ahvma.org, where you can search by state. Holistic vets can also be a great start for helping you identify any underlying health issues you may be concerned about before transitioning your dog to a homemade diet.

NUTRITION AND BEHAVIOR

In my experience with my own dogs and with clients and rescue dogs I've worked with, I've found that a satisfied dog is a less mischievous dog! I've noticed this amazing connection and have discovered that when my pets have adequate sustenance, they are less inclined to try to find it in inappropriate places and ways, like begging or picking through the garbage.

Diets that are nutritionally inadequate can affect a dog's behavior in a few ways. For example, a deficiency in fatty acids can cause depression. If you find your dog is acting aggressive, he might benefit from a decrease in protein and an increase in fat and carbohydrates. Both fats and carbohydrates have a calming effect on mood.

Feeding a homemade diet can help address many health and behavior issues and be an important building block for a healthier, happier dog.

ADDRESSING ALLERGIES

One of the main reasons my clients transition their dogs to a homemade diet is to combat skin or food allergies. Many dogs suffer from food allergies, in large part due to their diet and the fact that they are eating the same thing every day. Over time, many dogs develop allergies to commercial pet foods, especially if one of the main ingredients is always the same. Beyond that, kibble is dry and lacks moisture, which can lead to dry, itchy skin and constant scratching in certain dogs. It also lacks the ever-important essential fatty acids.

Some of the symptoms dogs may exhibit because of allergies include:

- Dry, itchy skin and constant scratching
- Hair loss
- Sneezing and coughing
- Dry, brittle coat
- Loose stool
- Itchy paws

I've seen amazing results from feeding both cooked and raw diets when it comes to addressing these types of symptoms.

THE BASICS OF A HOMEMADE DIET

A dog's diet must be composed of the proper amounts of animal protein, fat, and carbohydrates, as each of these macronutrients supports different bodily functions. Here's a breakdown of the essentials of a homemade dog diet:

ESSENTIAL NUTRIENTS

Animal Protein: Animal protein is necessary for growth, repairing tissue, and maintaining muscle mass. I use chicken, turkey, beef, lamb, jack mackerel, pork, tuna, salmon, sole, and anchovies in many of my recipes as sources of protein. You can also feed your dog duck and venison, although these proteins can be harder to find.

Fat: Fat is the most concentrated source of energy for dogs and provides essential fatty acids (EFAs), arachidonic acid, omega-3 fatty acid, and omega-6 fatty acid. Fat assists in the absorption of vitamins, supports the immune system, and is vital for healthy skin and coat. Organ meats are an excellent source of high-quality protein as well as essential fatty acids. Chicken and beef hearts, livers, kidneys, and gizzards are key ingredients in my recipes and in a homemade diet for dogs, but they're very rich, so my recipes call for them in small quantities.

Carbohydrates: Carbohydrates break down into glucose, which supports the nervous system. They provide energy, vitamins, minerals, and fiber that don't exist in proteins and fats. Carbs that are good for dogs include vegetables, brown rice, millet, oatmeal, quinoa, barley, couscous, and cornmeal, to name a few. Quinoa is a great grain- and gluten-free option, and I use it quite a bit in my recipes.

Vegetables: Vegetables are an important source of energy, vitamins, minerals, and fiber. I call for pureed vegetables in many of the recipes because pureeing in a food processor breaks down the vegetables' cellulose walls and allows for better absorption and digestion. Note that high-fiber vegetables can loosen stool, so always monitor your dog and adjust amounts as necessary.

Essential Fatty Acids: Fish oils are the best source of essential fatty acids. Signs of EFA deficiency in dogs include a dull/dry coat, dry itchy skin, lack of energy, and long healing from injury or illness. Adding a serving of EFA-rich cod-liver oil, salmon oil, flaxseed oil, coconut oil, sunflower seed oil, or safflower oil can help these symptoms.

Calcium: Calcium is one of the most important things to include in your dog's homemade diet. Some suppliers sell meat just for dogs, and a good supplier will sell meat that's human-grade but has 30 percent bone ground in. If you're using a meat with ground-in bone, you don't need a bonemeal supplement. If you can't find a supplier that sells meat with ground-in bone or a butcher who will do this for you, you should add a bonemeal supplement to your pet's food every day. A 50-pound dog should get about 1,000 mg of bonemeal supplement per day. Be sure to purchase a bonemeal supplement specifically for animals or humans, not bonemeal used for gardening. You can purchase bonemeal supplement at many health food and pet stores.

Bonemeal supplies calcium, but you can also make your own calcium supplement from eggshells if you want to take a more homemade approach (see page 24). The calcium in eggshells is calcium carbonate, and is not as easily absorbed as citrate, which can be purchased as a supplement. Calcium citrate is an ideal choice for dogs that need limited phosphorus in their diet, like dogs with kidney or renal problems.

Multivitamins: I highly recommend adding a multivitamin to your dog's meals, preferably one with probiotics. This is especially important if you won't be feeding your dog yogurt on a regular basis. I use a plant-based multivitamin that offers a complete package of essential vitamins and minerals, including:

- Vitamins A, C, D, E, and eight B vitamins
- Calcium, magnesium, chromium, zinc, copper, iodine, and manganese
- Friendly intestinal microflora—*Lactobacillus acidophilus*—plus prebiotics to support to promote a healthy immune system

Be sure to choose a multivitamin with all of the above vitamins and minerals.

There are certain additional foods that are very beneficial for dogs that can help with specific health issues, which I incorporate into many of my recipes. You do not have to use each of these ingredients every day, but you can add any of these to your dog's diet on a weekly rotation.

Yogurt: Yogurt with live cultures provides probiotics that help with digestion.

Parsley: This leafy green garnish helps combat bad breath and aids digestion. I like to add it to my dogs' meals a few times a week.

Garlic: There's a bit of a controversy about garlic and whether or not it's good for dogs. Some people think that because it's so close to the onion family and onions are bad for dogs, it shouldn't be given at all. I believe that in small amounts, it's great for things like inflammation and infection. It also helps combat fleas.

Pumpkin: Pumpkin helps with digestion, gas, bloating, and loose stool. It's low in calories so it's good for overweight dogs, too, and it's rich in fiber. You can use canned pure pumpkin (just make sure it's not pumpkin pie mix) or you can easily make your own puree (see page 57).

Wheat Germ: Wheat germ is the most nutrient-rich part of the wheat plant and is high in vitamins B and E, folic acid, essential fatty acids, and fiber.

BASIC FOOD CHART

Here's a quick glance at some of the foods in each category that are healthy and nutritious to include in your dog's meals.

Animal Protein	Vegetables	Fats	Carbohydrates	Extras
anchovies	artichoke hearts	beef hearts	barley	apple cider vinegar
beef	asparagus	chicken gizzards	brown rice	coconut
chicken	bananas	chicken livers	cornmeal/polenta	garlic
duck	beets	coconut oil	couscous	hard-boiled eggs
herring	broccoli	flaxseed oil	farro	parsley
lamb	Brussels sprouts	safflower oil	lentils	pumpkin
mackerel	carrots	salmon oil	millet	wheat germ
pork	cauliflower		oats/oatmeal	yogurt
salmon	celery		potatoes (sweet and regular)	
sardines	green beans		quinoa	
sole	kale		quinoa pasta	
swordfish	peas			
trout	spinach			
tuna	squash			
turkey	zucchini			
venison				

Hard-Boiled Eggs: Not only are eggs an excellent source of protein, they also provide all of a dog's essential amino acids. When hard-boiled and served with the shell on, as I call for in many of my recipes, the egg is also a good source of calcium.

EGGSHELLS AS A CALCIUM SUBSTITUTE

Bonemeal or calcium carbonate is an important element in a dog's diet. The easiest way to provide this is to give him raw meaty bones or raw meat that contains ground-in bone as part of his diet. If you are using raw meat that does not contain bone, it's important to provide calcium from another source, such as eggshells. You can add shell-on hard-boiled eggs to your dog's meals, but you can also make your own calcium supplement from just the eggshells. Here's how: Hard-boil a dozen eggs. Let cool, then peel the eggs, reserving the shells. Clean and dry the eggshells, then set them aside for 2 days to completely dry out. Place them on a baking sheet and cook at 300°F for 8 to 10 minutes. Remove them from the oven and let cool. Using a clean coffee grinder, grind the shells into powder, working in batches if necessary. This should yield about 12 tablespoons. Store the eggshell powder in an airtight container in a cool, dry place for up to 2 months. Use about ½ teaspoon per 1 cup of food (see feeding chart on pages 34–35) once a day.

I also use hard-boiled eggs with the shell on in a lot of my recipes, because both the egg and the shell provide nutritional value. When serving shell-on hard-boiled eggs with meals, follow these feeding guidelines:

5- to 20-pound dog	¼ egg/day
20- to 30-pound dog	½ egg/day
30- to 40-pound dog	1 egg/day
40- to 60-pound dog	1½ eggs/day
70- to 100-pound dog	2 eggs/day

Store hard-boiled eggs in an uncovered bowl in the refrigerator for up to 3 days.

Apple Cider Vinegar: Raw, unfiltered apple cider vinegar provides tremendous health benefits for dogs, just as it does for humans. Here are just a few:

- Helps alleviate itchy ears and feet by balancing a dog's natural pH level
- Reduces dander
- Relieves arthritis
- Improves digestion
- Prevents formation of kidney and bladder stones
- Serves as a natural insect repellant
- Eases muscle pain and soreness

Serving size for a 50-pound dog is 1 tablepoon per serving for optimal benefits.

Coconut: Coconut products such as milk, oil, and unsweetened flakes offer a wide range of health benefits for dogs, including a healthy coat and skin, improved digestion, and a balanced metabolism. They can also help reduce the risk of some cancers, and the oil can be used topically to treat minor cuts.

PORTIONS AND RATIOS

The ratio of meat to vegetables to fat to carbs that I use in my recipes closely replicates what a dog would eat in the wild. Ideally, your dog's meal should consist of the following:

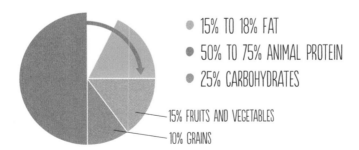

- 15% TO 18% FAT
- 50% TO 75% ANIMAL PROTEIN
- 25% CARBOHYDRATES

15% FRUITS AND VEGETABLES

10% GRAINS

These ratios should be adjusted slightly based on your dog's activity level. My dogs are very active, so I tend to give them a little more fat for extra energy, especially if I'm taking them on a long hike or if they're going for a good run on the beach. If your dog has any specific health issues, you should always consult your vet before feeding a homemade diet to make sure your dog gets the proper balanced diet for his specific needs.

FOODS YOUR DOG SHOULD NOT EAT

There are certain foods your dog should *never* eat. These include:

- **Grapes and Raisins:** It's not fully understood why, but grapes and raisins can cause life-threatening renal failure in dogs. Even a very small amount can be toxic.

- **Alcohol:** A dog's liver cannot metabolize alcohol and even a small amount can be very toxic.

- **Chocolate:** Chocolate contains theobromine, something dogs cannot process like humans can and which is therefore harmful.

- **Citrus:** Citrus fruits and other products can cause gastrointestinal irritation and central nervous system depression.

- **Seasoned Meats:** Meat spices used to enhance flavors, such as onion powder, can be very toxic to dogs as they are often loaded with preservatives and artificial ingredients.

- **Coffee and Grounds:** Like alcohol, caffeine—even in small amounts—can be toxic to dogs and adversely affect their central nervous system. This includes caffeine found in energy drinks, tea, coffee, chocolate, and coffee grounds.

- **Avocados:** The leaves, bark, and fruit of avocados contain persin, which is toxic to dogs.

- **Sugar:** Just like it does to us, sugar spikes a dog's blood-sugar levels and offers no nutritional value for them, so it should be avoided.

- **Grease:** Consumption of excess fatty grease from high-fat-content foods can cause diarrhea and vomiting.

- **Cooked Bones:** I feed my dogs raw marrow bones all the time, as they're excellent for their teeth and very nutritious. Never give your dog a cooked bone, however, since they can splinter and puncture the digestive system if swallowed.

- **Macadamia Nuts:** When even just a few are consumed, dogs can have a toxic reaction and experience an elevated heart rate, vomiting, and muscle tremors.

- **Onions:** The oils in onions contain an antioxidant that negatively affects hemoglobin in dogs' red blood cells.

- **Persimmons:** The seeds in these fruits can cause inflammation in the intestines.

- **Rawhide:** Rawhide treats are loaded with preservatives and additives and can be highly indigestible to dogs. They can also be a choking hazard.

- **Soy:** Soy is not readily digested by dogs and can cause gas and bloating.

ORGANIC VERSUS NON-ORGANIC

I try to use organic ingredients whenever possible because of the excessive amount of antibiotics, preservatives, pesticides, and additives used in and on non-organic meat and vegetables. I also like going to my local farmer's markets to buy locally grown seasonal vegetables. I try to think ahead and stock organic meat in my freezer so I always have it on hand. It's also important to use organic organ meat, if you can find it. In general, go organic and/or local whenever you can.

THE IMPORTANCE OF VARYING YOUR DOG'S MEALS

One of the most essential things about feeding your dog a homemade diet, or any diet for that matter, is varying your dog's meals. No one food can provide all of the macronutrients and micronutrients needed for a healthy, balanced diet. Feeding your pet one type of food over and over again can also lead to food allergies, and variety is essential to prevent nutritional deficiencies and hypersensitivities. I like to vary my dogs' meals every other day or every three days. And if I feed them chicken for a few days in a row, for instance, I try to feed them different carbs, fats, and vegetables each day.

CREATING YOUR CANINE KITCHEN

There are a few essential things you'll want to have on hand that will make cooking for your dog much easier. Most important is a food processor. I use it in almost all of my recipes because it breaks down the cellulose walls in vegetables and makes them more digestible. It also cuts down on chopping time and makes my life a bit easier! You don't need a large or expensive one; a small, 4-cup chopper/grinder will do the trick.

Here are some additional must-haves:

- Cutting board
- Plastic or glass storage containers for refrigerating and freezing
- Knives
- Kitchen scissors
- Assorted large pots and sauté pans
- 9½-by-13-inch baking dish
- Measuring cups and spoons
- Cooling rack
- 12-cup muffin tin
- Baking sheet
- Small food scale
- Pot holders

- Mixing bowls and spoons
- Aluminum foil

TIPS AND SHORTCUTS FOR PREPPING, COOKING, AND STORAGE

There are a few simple things you can do and shortcuts you can take to cut down on time spent shopping and cooking. To prep for the week, I suggest setting aside one day during the week to shop, and then two days a week to cook. I choose Sundays to shop and cook and Wednesday evenings as my second cooking day. If you're not going to freeze anything, you'll need to cook every three days to keep the ingredients fresh. Here are some additional suggestions:

Plan meals ahead of time. I buy meat for my dogs through a local distributor called Armellino's, located in Huntington, New York, and they sell meat specifically for dogs. For things like organ meat, vegetables, canned jack mackerel, and tuna, I watch for what's on sale at the grocery store and then plan my meals for the week. Writing a shopping list is also a big help.

Chop vegetables ahead of time. On your dedicated cooking days, chop and/or puree all the vegetables you'll need for that part of the week and store them in separate airtight containers in the refrigerator. These can be used for three days. You can also freeze them and defrost them as needed throughout the week.

Buy in bulk. With four dogs, I have to buy in bulk to save money and time; otherwise I'd be running out to the store every day. I love shopping at wholesale clubs like Costco and Sam's Club and stocking up on items such as:
- Olive oil
- Couscous, rice, quinoa, millet, barley
- Canned tuna and chicken
- Frozen vegetables, for when you're in a pinch
- Frozen chicken breasts, fish, and other proteins
- Storage containers

Portion, then freeze. Since I have to make many meals a week for clients and feed four of my own dogs, I make one to two trips a month to Armellino's and buy a variety of meats in bulk. I then portion out ½- and 1-pound containers, label, and freeze them, so different quantities are easily accessible and easy to defrost.

Proper defrosting is very important. Always allow food to defrost in the refrigerator for twenty-four hours before serving to ensure it has thawed. If you have to microwave, don't microwave in plastic storage containers—I use microwave-safe glass bowls—and never microwave your dog's dish, especially if it's stainless steel. Allow the food to cool to room temperature before serving anything that was microwaved.

SANITATION

The same rules of sanitation that we follow as humans apply to the food you prep and cook for your pet. Here are some guidelines:

Have separate supplies for meat. I have a separate set of plastic storage containers, glass storage containers, kitchen scissors, cutting boards, and knives that I use only for handling raw meat for dog meals. This prevents cross-contamination. Never use the same cutting board for your dog's meat as the one you use for vegetables or anything you cook for yourself. Always wash anything that touched raw meat in hot water and soap before reusing.

Label and date everything. This is especially important if you're storing food in the refrigerator and not freezing it. The general rule of thumb is meat and vegetables can be stored in the refrigerator for three days, and anything older than that shouldn't be served to your dog. I use white masking tape and a permanent marker to label everything with the type of food, its weight, and the date it was made.

Now that we've gotten the basics down, let's move on to making those delicious homemade cooked meals.

CHAPTER 2

HOMEMADE
COOKED MEALS

WHEN TRANSITIONING YOUR DOG TO A HOME-COOKED DIET, I recommend doing so over a three- to four-week period. When I work with clients, I create a transition diet that ensures a gradual adjustment period for both the owner and the dog. During week one, I suggest adding some cooked meat—either chicken, turkey, or beef—to your dog's commercial pet food. For example, if your dog eats 1 cup of dry food at each meal, you would feed ¼ cup cooked meat and ¾ cup dry food for each meal. Here's a general ratio guideline for transitioning:

WEEK 1	¼ cooked meat, ¾ commercial food
WEEK 2	½ cooked meat, ½ commercial food
WEEK 3	¾ cooked meat, ¼ commercial food
WEEK 4	fully transitioned (if your dog needs one more week to transition, repeat week 3)

By week four, your dog should be fully transitioned to a homemade diet and you can start incorporating home-cooked carbs and veggies with the meat. As each transition is a function of your pet's age, health, and activity level, you should always talk to a vet first to rule out underlying health issues that need to be addressed before making this change.

THE DETOX PROCESS

It is important to note that your dog will experience a detox process that occurs when you transition from commercial pet food to a homemade diet. Canned pumpkin is a very good addition to your dog's meals to help ease the transition because it alleviates gas and bloating and helps with an upset stomach. I also suggest adding only small amounts of cooked vegetables initially, because vegetables can loosen the stool. Cooked vegetables are easier to digest than raw vegetables, so you may substitute cooked for raw in any of the recipes in this chapter. Lightly cooking vegetables breaks down their cellulose walls, making them easier to digest. Cooking vegetables with high heat does deplete nutrients, but this is okay through the transition process. As your dog's digestive system adjusts to a home-cooked meal, he will be able to tolerate raw vegetables, which have more nutrients.

As you transition you dog off of commercial pet food, you should closely monitor his behavior for changes that might indicate he is not tolerating the new diet. Signs such as lethargy, vomiting, diarrhea, decreased appetite, or excessive biting, itching, or scratching of the tail or

paws indicates that your pet may not be tolerating the transition well and you should talk to your vet.

IT'S NOT ALL OR NOTHING

Two important things to remember about feeding a homemade diet: It's not all or nothing, and variation is key. As I mentioned in Chapter 1, varying your dog's meals every few days will ensure he doesn't develop allergies. Dogs are natural scavengers and in the wild, they do not get the same meal every day or even all of the nutrients they need every day, but instead over the course of a short amount of time they consume all nutrients they require. This leads to the next point: Don't get too hung up on giving your dog everything every day. In many of my recipes, I suggest adding things like yogurt, wheat germ, parsley, and organ meat, but these don't need to be added to every recipe and can be given a few times a week instead. Some dogs may not tolerate vegetables at every meal, but you can include them once a day or once every other day.

Just remember not to take an all-or-nothing approach. You and your dog are learning a new routine. Use the recipes and guidelines in this book to make this an enjoyable learning experience.

BASIC FEEDING GUIDELINES

The recipes and serving sizes are based on a fifty-pound dog with an average activity level. Each serving size, which is one meal, should be adjusted accordingly with respect to your pet's weight, age, and activity level, using the feeding chart on pages 34–35 as a guideline. Because serving sizes depend on all of these factors, you should use your best judgment to determine what serving size is best for your dog, realizing that it may take time to find the right balance.

The recipes in this book are measured several ways. With the exception of the fishcakes and burgers, the recipes either call for ingredients to be combined to make one serving or for the entire serving size to be measured in cups. For the combined ingredients, you'll need to refer to the amount per serving for meat, vegetable, carbohydrate, organ meat, and extras columns in the serving size chart to determine how much of each ingredient to serve based on your dog's weight. A removable bookmark at the front of the book lists all the serving size charts for quick-and-easy reference while you're prepping and cooking.

Lastly, the measurements of vegetables and uncooked carbs that are called for are as accurate as possible so they yield the quantities you will need of the cooked and pureed versions. You may have extra of both.

SERVING SIZE CHART

	1	2	3
Dog's weight in pounds	Amount per serving for cooked recipes	Amount per serving of meat	Vegetables per serving
3–5	¼ cup–⅓ cup	2–3 Tbs.	¼–½ Tsp.
5–10	⅓ cup–½ cup	¼–⅓ cup	¼–½ Tsp.
10–20	½ cup–¾ cup	½–¾ cup	½–1 Tsp.
20–30	¾ cup–1 cup	½–¾ cup	1–1½ Tsp.
30–40	1 cup–1½ cups	¾–1 cup	2–3 Tsp.
40–50	1½ cups–2 cups	¾–1 cup	1–2 Tbs.
50–60	2 cups–2¼ cups	1–1½ cups	1–2 Tbs.
60–70	2¼ cups–2½ cups	1–1½ cups	2–3 Tbs.
70–80	2½ cups–2¾ cups	1½–2 cups	3 Tbs.–¼ cup
80–100	2¾ cups–3¼ cups	1½–2 cups	¼ cup–⅓ cup

I list a large range of vegetables serving sizes in the feeding chart, as certain dogs may not be able to tolerate or need as many vegetables as others. Anything within the range is suitable for a dog at the specified weight.

Always bear in mind that each dog is different and should be treated as an individual. Caloric requirements vary as they are a function of your dog's age, health status, and activity level. If you notice your dog is gaining weight, increase her activity level or cut back on how much you are feeding her. Conversely, if your dog seems to be losing weight or constantly looking for more food, you may have to increase how much you are feeding her. Always use your best judgment.

Finally, for recipes that call for separate ingredients to be mixed together for each serving, it's important to store the prepared ingredients in the refrigerator in separate airtight containers, and then mix those ingredients together for each serving at each meal. This ensures that you can monitor the freshness of individual ingredients, especially organ meat, as it tends to have a shorter shelf life than other ingredients. Never serve food that's more than three days old; adjust the amount you make and store accordingly.

4	5	6	7	8	9
Carbohydrates per serving	Organ meat per serving	Fishcakes per serving	Burgers per serving	Hard-boiled eggs *per day*	Extras* per serving
1–2 Tsp.	¼–½ Tsp.	¼	¼	¼ egg	¼ Tsp.
2 Tsp.–1 Tbs.	¼–½ Tsp.	⅓	½	¼ egg	½ Tsp.
1–2 Tbs.	½–1 Tsp.	½	¾	¼ egg	1 Tsp.
2–3 Tbs.	½–1 Tsp.	¾	1	½ egg	2 Tsp.
3 Tbs.–¼ cup	1–1½ Tsp.	1	1½	1 egg	½–1 Tbs.
¼ cup–⅓ cup	2 Tsp.–1 Tbs.	1½	1½	1½ eggs	1 Tbs.
⅓ cup–½ cup	2 Tsp.–1 Tbs.	1½	2	1½ eggs	1–1½ Tbs.
⅓ cup–½ cup	1½ Tbs.–2 Tbs.	1¾	2	2 eggs	1½–2 Tbs.
½ cup–¾ cup	1½ Tbs.–2 Tbs.	2	2½	2 eggs	1½–2 Tbs.
½ cup–¾ cup	2–2½ Tbs.	2	2½	2 eggs	2 Tbs.

* Extras include yogurt, wheat germ, flaxseed meal, oils, pumpkin, apple cider vinegar, and cottage cheese. Anchovies, mackerel, and sardines are considered extras for recipes in the raw recipes chapter.

I prefer to feed my dogs twice a day, with a snack in between meals. Feeding one large meal once a day places a lot of strain on your dog's digestive system, while feeding twice a day spreads the food out so your dog is not ravenous come meal time. Hunger can trigger aggressiveness and part of being a responsible dog owner is knowing what works best for your pet.

Here is a basic grocery list of all the things you'll need and want to stock up on:

- Raw meat
- Organ meat like beef hearts, chicken livers, or chicken gizzards
- Vegetables like carrots, celery, broccoli, and peas
- Quinoa, rice, barley, millet, and couscous
- Apple cider vinegar
- Parsley
- Yogurt
- Wheat germ
- Eggs
- Canned pumpkin (not pie filling—100% pure pumpkin)
- EFA supplements like fish oil
- Bonemeal supplement
- Multivitamin

GRILLED CHICKEN, BROWN RICE, AND BEETS

MAKES 4 SERVINGS FOR A 50-POUND DOG

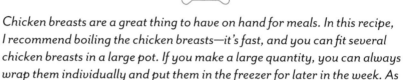

Chicken breasts are a great thing to have on hand for meals. In this recipe, I recommend boiling the chicken breasts—it's fast, and you can fit several chicken breasts in a large pot. If you make a large quantity, you can always wrap them individually and put them in the freezer for later in the week. As another time saver, you can buy precooked packaged beets and skip the boiling process.

2½ pounds boneless, skinless chicken breasts

¾ cup uncooked brown rice

1 small beet

1 Place the chicken breasts in a large pot with enough water to cover them completely. Bring the water to a boil, then reduce the heat to medium-high and cook for 15 to 20 minutes, until the chicken is cooked through. Set it aside to cool. Once the chicken has cooled, dice it and set it aside.

2 Prepare the rice as directed on the package and set it aside to cool. You should have about 2 cups of cooked rice.

3 Place the beet in a saucepan with enough water to cover. Bring the water to a boil, then reduce to a simmer and cook for about 45 minutes, or until the beet is tender. Set it aside. Once cooled, peel the beet, then dice it and puree it in a food processor. You should have about ¼ cup of beet puree.

TO MAKE ONE SERVING

1½ cups cooked chicken

½ cup cooked brown rice

1 tablespoon beet puree

In your dog's bowl, combine the chicken, rice, and beet puree and mix well to combine. Refer to the feeding chart on pages 34–35, columns 2, 3, and 4, and adjust according to your dog's weight. Refrigerate any leftovers in an airtight container for up to 3 days.

GROUND BEEF, COUSCOUS, AND BROCCOLI

MAKES 4 SERVINGS FOR A 50-POUND DOG

When you're first learning to cook homemade meals for your dog, it's best to start simple. It's important to get used to the many different food combinations and ratios that are standard in homemade meals for dogs (see pages 34–35). Starting out with simple ingredients and recipes also gives your dog a chance to discover his taste buds and decide what he likes and doesn't like. Once you get comfortable with the general guidelines, you can feel free to experiment with different kinds of meats and vegetables. I bet your dog will be a willing taste tester!

1 tablespoon olive oil	1 cup uncooked couscous
2 pounds ground beef	¼ cup chopped broccoli florets

1   In a large sauté pan, heat the oil over medium-low heat. Add the beef and cook until it is browned. Drain any excess fat and set it aside to cool.

2   Prepare the couscous as directed on the package and set it aside to cool. You should have about 2 cups of cooked couscous.

3   Puree the broccoli in a food processor and set it aside. You should have about ¼ cup of broccoli puree.

TO MAKE ONE SERVING

1 ⅓ cups cooked beef	1 tablespoon pureed broccoli
½ cup cooked couscous	

In your dog's bowl, combine the beef, couscous, and broccoli puree and mix well to combine. Refer to the feeding chart on pages 34–35, columns 2, 3, and 4, and adjust according to your dog's size. Refrigerate any leftovers in an airtight container for up to 3 days.

GROUND TURKEY, QUINOA, AND CARROTS

MAKES 4 SERVINGS FOR A 50-POUND DOG

Quinoa is one of my favorite carbs to make for my dogs. They love it, and I can make a lot at once because it lasts for several days. With four dogs, it's hard to have any leftovers, but quinoa is very easy to buy, make, and store in bulk. For added variety I also cook red quinoa and tricolor quinoa.

1 tablespoon olive oil

2 pounds ground turkey

1 cup uncooked quinoa

¼ cup chopped carrot

1. In a large sauté pan, heat the oil over medium-low heat. Add the turkey and cook until it is browned. Drain any excess fat and set it aside to cool.

2. Cook the quinoa as directed on the package and set it aside to cool. You should have about 2 cups of cooked quinoa.

3. Puree the carrot in a food processor. You should have about ¼ cup of carrot puree.

TO MAKE ONE SERVING

1⅓ cups cooked turkey

½ cup cooked quinoa

1 tablespoon pureed carrots

In your dog's bowl, combine the turkey, quinoa, and carrot puree and mix well to combine. Refer to the feeding chart on pages 34–35, columns 2, 3, and 4, and adjust according to your dog's size. Refrigerate any leftovers in an airtight container for up to 3 days.

GROUND PORK, MILLET, AND CELERY

MAKE 4 SERVINGS FOR A 50-POUND DOG

Millet is another good carb for dogs because it's rich in B vitamins and is higher in protein than most other grains. It's also a great source of magnesium, phosphorus, and fiber and is gluten free—a good choice for dogs that have a food sensitivity. Like quinoa, millet is easy to buy and make in bulk and my dogs just eat it right up. If you cannot find millet in your grocery store, you can easily substitute another carb like quinoa or barley, which also have a high fiber content.

1 tablespoon olive oil	¾ cup uncooked millet
2 pounds ground pork	¾ cups diced celery

1. In a large sauté pan, heat the oil over medium-low heat. Add the pork and cook until it is browned. Drain any excess fat and set it aside to cool.

2. Cook the millet as directed on the package and set it aside to cool. You should have about 2 cups of cooked millet.

3. Puree the celery in a food processor. You should have about ¼ cup of celery puree.

TO MAKE ONE SERVING

1⅓ cups cooked pork	1 tablespoon pureed celery
½ cup cooked millet	

In your dog's bowl, combine the pork, millet, and celery puree. Refer to the feeding chart on pages 34–35, columns 2, 3, and 4, and adjust according to your dog's weight. Refrigerate any leftovers in an airtight container for up to 3 days.

TURKEY, EGGS, AND YOGURT

MAKES 4 SERVINGS FOR A 50-POUND DOG

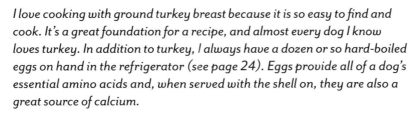

I love cooking with ground turkey breast because it is so easy to find and cook. It's a great foundation for a recipe, and almost every dog I know loves turkey. In addition to turkey, I always have a dozen or so hard-boiled eggs on hand in the refrigerator (see page 24). Eggs provide all of a dog's essential amino acids and, when served with the shell on, they are also a great source of calcium.

1 tablespoon olive oil

2 pounds ground turkey breast

¼ cup chopped carrot

4 hard-boiled eggs, shell on
(see page 24)

¼ cup plain yogurt containing live
active cultures

¼ cup wheat germ

1 In a large sauté pan, heat the oil over medium-low heat. Add the turkey and cook until browned. Drain any excess fat and set the turkey aside to cool.

2 Puree the carrots in a food processor. You should have about ¼ cup of carrot puree.

TO MAKE ONE SERVING

1⅓ cups cooked turkey breast

1 hard-boiled egg, shell on, cut in half
or chopped into small pieces

1 tablespoon yogurt

1 tablespoon pureed carrots

1 tablespoon wheat germ

In your dog's bowl, combine the turkey, egg, yogurt, carrot puree, and wheat germ. Refer to the feeding chart on pages 34–35, columns 2, 3, 8, and 9, and adjust according to your dog's weight. Refrigerate any leftovers in an airtight container for up to 3 days.

SPAGHETTI BOLOGNESE

MAKES 4 SERVINGS FOR A 50-POUND DOG

Whenever I make pasta for myself, I always cook an extra box and make this recipe for my dogs. Any time I can make something for myself and for them, I do—since it's a big time saver. In this dog-friendly recipe, I use gluten-free quinoa pasta, which provides significantly more protein than traditional wheat pastas, and is a good alternative for dogs who have a slight sensitivity to wheat.

1 tablespoon olive oil

2 pounds ground beef

1 cup uncooked quinoa pasta

¼ cup (2 ounces) chopped chicken liver

⅔ cup diced zucchini

1 In a large sauté pan, heat the oil over medium-low heat. Add the beef and cook until it is browned. Drain any excess fat and set it aside to cool.

2 Prepare the pasta as directed on the package. Drain and set it aside to cool. You should have about 2 cups of cooked pasta.

3 Puree the zucchini in a food processor. You should have about ¼ cup of zucchini puree.

TO MAKE ONE SERVING

1⅓ cups cooked beef

½ cup cooked pasta

1 tablespoon chopped chicken liver

1 tablespoon pureed zucchini

In your dog's bowl, combine the beef, pasta, liver, and zucchini puree. Refer to the feeding chart on pages 34–35, columns 2, 3, 4, and 5, and adjust according to your dog's weight. Refrigerate any leftovers in an airtight container for up to 3 days.

TUNA STEAK AND POTATOES
MAKES 4 SERVINGS FOR A 50-POUND DOG

Tuna is very healthy for dogs in a regulated amount, as it's rich in muscle-building protein and omega-3 fatty acids and low in fat. Because it has higher mercury levels than other types of fish, your dog shouldn't have tuna every day, but a few times a month is fine. Tuna steaks can be expensive, too, so this is a meal I make sporadically. When I can find tuna steaks on sale, I buy them in bulk and freeze them. If you can't find tuna steaks, you can substitute canned tuna, but be sure to buy tuna packed in water and not in oil.

1¼ pounds tuna steak

2 cups diced red potatoes, skin on

¼ cup (2 ounces) chopped beef heart

¼ cup canned pure pumpkin

1 In a large pot, cover the tuna with water and set over medium-high heat. Cook for 15 to 20 minutes, until the tuna is cooked through. Drain and set the tuna aside to cool.

2 Bring a large pot of water to a boil. Add the potatoes and cook them for 20 minutes, or until they are soft. Drain and set them aside to cool.

3 Once the tuna is cooled, cut it into bite-size pieces or coarsely chop it in a food processor.

TO MAKE ONE SERVING

1⅓ cups cooked tuna

½ cup cooked potatoes

1 tablespoon chopped beef heart

1 tablespoon canned pure pumpkin

In your dog's bowl, combine the tuna, potatoes, beef heart, and pumpkin. Refer to the feeding chart on pages 34–35, columns 2, 3, 4, and 5, and and adjust according to your dog's weight. Refrigerate any leftovers in an airtight container for up to 3 days.

CHOP-LICKING PORK CHOPS
MAKES 4 SERVINGS FOR A 50-POUND DOG

I cook pork loin for my dogs a lot, and as you'll see, I use it in a lot of my treat recipes, too. My dogs love pork loin (and so do my cats!), so this is an easy thing for me to make that lasts several meals. Seasonings like onion powder can be toxic to dogs, so the pork loin should be cooked with no seasoning.

About 1½ pounds boneless pork loin

¾ cup uncooked brown rice

¼ cup chopped broccoli florets

¼ cup plain yogurt containing live active cultures

1 Preheat the oven to 350°F. Cook the pork loin in a baking dish, covered with foil, for about 45 minutes, or until the middle is no longer pink. Remove it from the oven and set it aside to cool.

2 Cook the brown rice as directed on the package and set it aside. You should have about 2 cups of brown rice.

3 Puree the broccoli in a food processor and set it aside. You should have about ¼ cup of broccoli puree.

4 Once the pork loin is cool, chop it into bite-size pieces or coarsely chop it in a food processor.

TO MAKE ONE SERVING

1⅓ cups cooked pork loin

½ cup cooked brown rice

1 tablespoon pureed broccoli

1 tablespoon plain yogurt

In your dog's bowl, combine the pork, rice, broccoli puree, and yogurt. Refer to the feeding chart on pages 34–35, columns 2, 3, 4, and 9, and adjust according to your dog's weight. Refrigerate any leftovers in an airtight container for up to 3 days.

K9 QUICHE
MAKES 6 TO 7 SERVINGS FOR A 50-POUND DOG

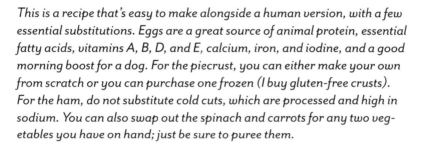

This is a recipe that's easy to make alongside a human version, with a few essential substitutions. Eggs are a great source of animal protein, essential fatty acids, vitamins A, B, D, and E, calcium, iron, and iodine, and a good morning boost for a dog. For the piecrust, you can either make your own from scratch or you can purchase one frozen (I buy gluten-free crusts). For the ham, do not substitute cold cuts, which are processed and high in sodium. You can also swap out the spinach and carrots for any two vegetables you have on hand; just be sure to puree them.

1 (9-inch) homemade or store-bought piecrust

1 cup chopped spinach

¼ cup chopped carrots

4 large eggs

3 cups cubed ham steak

2 cups shredded part-skim mozzarella cheese

¼ cup (2 ounces) chopped beef heart

2 tablespoons unsalted beef broth

¼ cup wheat germ

1 Preheat the oven to 400°F.

2 Spray a 9-inch pie dish with nonstick cooking spray. Line the dish with your piecrust.

3 Puree the spinach in a food processor and set it aside. You should have about ¼ cup of spinach puree. Then puree the carrots in a food processor and set them aside. You should have about ¼ cup of carrot puree.

4 In a large bowl, beat the eggs. Add the ham, cheese, pureed vegetables, beef heart, and broth, and mix well.

5 Pour the entire mixture into the piecrust and top it with the wheat germ.

6 Cover the pie with foil and bake it for 35 to 40 minutes, until the center is set. Let the quiche cool completely before serving.

7 Chop the quiche into bite-size pieces. To make one serving, refer to column 1 of the feeding chart on pages 34–35, and measure in cups according to your dog's weight. Refrigerate any leftovers in an airtight container for up to 3 days.

EASY AS POTPIE
MAKES 6 TO 7 SERVINGS FOR A 50-POUND DOG

Ground chicken is a good meat to stock in your freezer. If you cannot find it already ground, you can ask your butcher to grind 1½ pounds of chicken cutlets for you. I like to divide it into 1-pound patties and store them in separate containers so they're already portioned and easy to grab and defrost. It's also easier to defrost smaller amounts than large, so portioning the meat before you freeze it will speed up the defrosting time.

2 (9-inch) homemade or store-bought piecrusts

2 cups frozen or canned peas

1 cup chopped carrots

1½ pounds ground chicken

1 large egg

1 Preheat the oven to 400°F.

2 Spray a 9-inch pie dish with nonstick cooking spray. Line the dish with one piecrust.

3 Cook the frozen peas according to the package directions. Once they've cooled (or if using canned), puree them in a food processor. You should have about 1 cup of pea puree.

4 Add the carrots to the food processor and puree. You should have about 1 cup of carrot puree.

5 In a large bowl, mix together the peas, carrots, chicken, and egg. Pour the mixture into the piecrust and cover it with the remaining piecrust. Seal and crimp the edges together.

6 Cover the pie with foil. Bake it for 30 to 35 minutes, or until the top piecrust is golden brown. Remove it from the oven and let it cool completely before serving.

7 Chop the pie into bite-size pieces. To make one serving, refer to column 1 of the feeding chart on pages 34–35 and measure in cups according to your dog's weight. Refrigerate any leftovers in an airtight container for up to 3 days.

SHEPHERD'S PIE

MAKES 7 TO 8 SERVINGS FOR A 50-POUND DOG

You can use any ground meat for this recipe, it doesn't have to be lamb. For the potatoes, I usually leave the skin on because it provides more nutrition. If your dog is fussy about eating the skins, cut them up into very small pieces or chop them in a food processor.

½ cup unsalted beef broth

2 pounds ground lamb

½ cup frozen or canned peas

½ cup chopped carrot

6 medium red potatoes, diced

1. Preheat the oven to 400°F.

2. In a large saucepan, simmer the lamb in the broth over medium-low heat until browned.

3. Add the peas and carrot to the lamb and simmer for another 2 to 3 minutes to soften the vegetables.

4. In a medium pot, cover the potatoes with water and bring them to a boil. Cook them until they are soft when pierced with the tip of a knife, about 25 minutes. Drain them and mash well in the pot.

5. Spray a 9-by-13-inch baking dish with nonstick cooking spray. Pour the lamb and vegetable mixture into the prepared baking dish and distribute the mashed potatoes evenly over top.

6. Cover with foil and bake the pie for 15 minutes, removing the foil for the last 5 minutes. Remove it from the oven and let it cool completely before serving.

7. To make one serving, refer to column 1 of the feeding chart on pages 34–35 and measure in cups according to your dog's weight. Refrigerate any leftovers in an airtight container for up to 3 days.

SLOPPY JOES
MAKES 6 SERVINGS FOR A 50-POUND DOG

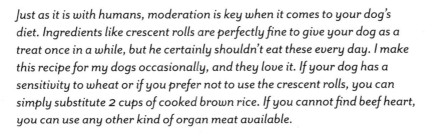

Just as it is with humans, moderation is key when it comes to your dog's diet. Ingredients like crescent rolls are perfectly fine to give your dog as a treat once in a while, but he certainly shouldn't eat these every day. I make this recipe for my dogs occasionally, and they love it. If your dog has a sensitivity to wheat or if you prefer not to use the crescent rolls, you can simply substitute 2 cups of cooked brown rice. If you cannot find beef heart, you can use any other kind of organ meat available.

1 (8-ounce) container crescent rolls	⅓ cup wheat germ
4 cups chopped fresh spinach	¼ cup (2 ounces) chopped beef heart
1 pound ground beef	1 large egg

1 Preheat the oven to 350°F.

2 Spray a 9-inch round baking dish with nonstick cooking spray. Line the dish with the crescent rolls.

3 Steam the spinach over simmering water just until it wilts, about 3 minutes. Roughly chop it.

4 In a large bowl, combine the spinach, beef, wheat germ, beef heart, and egg. Mix thoroughly. Spread the mixture evenly over the crescent rolls.

5 Cover the baking dish with foil. Bake the pie for 30–35 minutes, until the meat is cooked through. Remove it from the oven and let cool completely before serving.

6 To make one serving, refer to column 1 of the feeding chart on pages 34–35 and measure in cups according to your dog's weight. Refrigerate any leftovers in an airtight container for up to 3 days.

POTLUCK POLENTA
MAKES 10 SERVINGS FOR A 50-POUND DOG

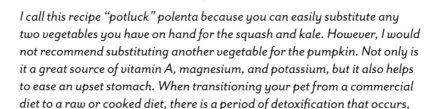

I call this recipe "potluck" polenta because you can easily substitute any two vegetables you have on hand for the squash and kale. However, I would not recommend substituting another vegetable for the pumpkin. Not only is it a great source of vitamin A, magnesium, and potassium, but it also helps to ease an upset stomach. When transitioning your pet from a commercial diet to a raw or cooked diet, there is a period of detoxification that occurs, and I find that adding pumpkin to some meals helps ease the transition.

1 cup chopped fresh kale

1 cup diced yellow squash

2 pounds precooked polenta

2 pounds ground beef

1 (15-ounce) can jack mackerel, drained

½ cup canned pure pumpkin

1 Preheat the oven to 350°F.

2 Steam the kale over simmering water until it is tender, about 5 minutes. Drain it, then puree it in a food processor and set aside. You should have about ½ cup of kale puree.

3 Puree the squash in a food processor and set it aside as well. You should have about ½ cup of squash puree.

4 Coat the bottom of an 9-by-13-inch casserole or baking dish with nonstick cooking spray. Using a spatula, spread half of the polenta evenly over the entire bottom of the dish.

5 Layer the beef on top of the polenta. Spread the pumpkin, kale puree, and squash puree on top of the beef. Add the mackerel and then spread the remaining polenta on top.

6 Cover the dish with foil and bake for 25 minutes. Remove the casserole from the oven and let it cool completely before serving.

7 To make one serving, refer to column 1 of the feeding chart on pages 34–35 and measure in cups according to your dog's weight. Store any leftovers in an airtight container for up to 3 days.

MADDIE'S MASH

MAKES 10 SERVINGS FOR A 50-POUND DOG

My thirteen-year-old shepherd mix, Maddie, has been on a cooked and raw diet ever since I rescued her twelve years ago. She's still a very active dog, and this is a very nutritious meal that helps keep all my dogs fit.

1½ pounds medium red potatoes, diced

1½ cups chickpea flour

1 cup hot water

1¼ cups unsalted chicken broth

1 cup frozen or canned peas

1 cup chopped broccoli florets

6 hard-boiled eggs, shells on (see page 24)

2 pounds ground beef

1 Preheat the oven to 375°F. Coat a 9-by-13-inch baking dish with nonstick cooking spray.

2 In a medium pot, cover the potatoes with water and bring to a boil. Cook until the potatoes are soft when pierced with the tip of a knife, about 25 minutes. Drain and mash well in the pot.

3 In a large bowl, combine the flour and water. Mix until the batter is smooth. Add the mashed potatoes and broth, mix well, and set aside.

4 In a food processor, puree the peas and set them aside. Repeat with the broccoli. You should have about 1 cup each of pureed broccoli and peas.

5 Roughly chop the hard-boiled eggs, with the shells on, in the food processor; set them aside.

6 Spread half of the mashed potato mixture evenly over the bottom of the prepared baking dish. Layer the ground beef on top, then layer the vegetables on top of the beef, and then layer on the chopped eggs. Cover the eggs with the remaining potato mixture.

7 Cover the dish with foil and bake for 30 minutes. Refrigerate the casserole for 1 hour before serving.

8 To make one serving, refer to column 1 of the feeding chart on pages 34–35 and measure in cups according to your dog's weight. Refrigerate any leftovers in an airtight container for up to 3 days.

SALMON BAKE
MAKES 6 TO 7 SERVINGS FOR A 50-POUND DOG

Salmon is an excellent source of omega-3 fatty acids and protein. It also helps improve a dog's coat, maintains heart health, and provides a great energy boost. It's very important to make sure it's cooked thoroughly, as serving undercooked salmon can cause serious illness in dogs. You'll also want to make sure that the salmon doesn't have any bones in it before adding it to this recipe. While you can use canned salmon for this recipe, fresh is always a healthier option because the canned salmon may contain preservatives and additives.

1 pound raw salmon

1 tablespoon extra-virgin olive oil

1 pound frozen chopped spinach

1⅓ cups uncooked brown rice

1 large egg

3 tablespoons canned pure pumpkin

2 (15-ounce) cans jack mackerel, drained

¼ cup wheat germ

1 Preheat the oven to 375°F. Coat the bottom of a 9-by-13-inch casserole dish with nonstick cooking spray.

2 By hand or in a food processor, chop the salmon into small, bite-size pieces and set them aside. Use a fork to comb through the salmon and pick out any bones.

3 In a large sauté pan, heat the oil over medium-low heat. Add the spinach and cook until it is completely defrosted. Drain it well and set aside.

4 Prepare the rice as directed on the package. Set the cooked rice aside. You should have about 4 cups of cooked rice.

5 In a large bowl, combine the rice, egg, and pumpkin and mix well. Set aside.

6 In a separate bowl, combine the mackerel and salmon and mix well. Set aside.

7 Spread the rice mixture evenly over the bottom of the prepared casserole dish. Next, evenly spread the fish mixture on top of the rice. Add the chopped spinach. Sprinkle the top of the casserole with the wheat germ.

8 Cover the dish with foil and bake for 30 minutes. Let the casserole cool completely before serving.

9 To make one serving, refer to column 1 of the feeding chart on pages 34–35 and measure in cups according to your dog's weight. Refrigerate any leftovers in an airtight container for up to 3 days.

MAKING YOUR OWN PUMPKIN PUREE

When pumpkins are in season, mostly in the fall and winter, it's very easy to make your own pumpkin puree (when you can't make your own, use canned). You'll want to choose a healthy-looking pumpkin that doesn't have many blemishes. I like to use several small pumpkins, because they're easier to handle and they fit on my cookie sheets. Here are the steps:

1. Preheat the oven to 350°F.

2. Cut the pumpkin in half and then slice off the stem.

3. Using a spoon, clean out the insides.

4. Line a cookie sheet with parchment paper and place the halves face down.

5. Brush the tops of the pumpkin with olive oil to avoid drying.

6. Bake for 45–55 minutes, until very soft on the outside.

7. Remove from the oven and allow to cool, then scoop out the insides with a spoon. Store the puree in an airtight container for up to 1 week.

CHICKEN MAC 'N' CHEESE
MAKES 6 TO 8 SERVINGS FOR A 50-POUND DOG

Mac and cheese is the ultimate comfort food. I developed this protein-filled dog-friendly version, and they just love it. I use whatever organ meat I have on hand for this recipe—beef hearts, chicken gizzards, or chicken livers—all of which are rich in nutrients and provide the necessary 15 percent fat that each canine meal should include.

1 pound uncooked elbow macaroni

2 cups shredded part-skim
mozzarella cheese

¼ cup low-fat milk

1 tablespoon butter

1 small sweet potato, diced

2½ pounds ground chicken

¼ cup wheat germ

½ cup plain Greek yogurt

½ cup chopped beef heart

1 Preheat the oven to 350°F. Coat the bottom of a 9-by-13-inch casserole dish with nonstick cooking spray.

2 Cook the macaroni as directed on the package. Drain, then place it in a large bowl. Add the cheese, milk, and butter. Mix all the ingredients together until the cheese is melted.

3 In a medium pot, cover the sweet potato with water and bring it to a boil. Cook it until it is soft when pierced with the tip of a knife, about 20 minutes. Drain and mash well in the pot.

4 In a second bowl, combine the ground chicken and sweet potato.

5 Spread the macaroni and cheese mixture evenly over the bottom of the prepared dish. Spread the ground chicken and sweet potato mixture on top. Sprinkle with the wheat germ.

6 Cover the casserole with foil and bake it for 40 minutes, or until the chicken is fully cooked. Let the casserole cool completely.

7 To make one serving, refer to column 1 of the feeding chart on pages 34–35 and measure in cups according to your dog's weight. Add 1 tablespoon of the yogurt and 1 tablespoon of the organ meat to each serving (refer to columns 5 and 9 to adjust accordingly). Refrigerate leftovers in an airtight container for up to 3 days.

FIDO'S FISHCAKES
MAKES 5 SERVINGS FOR A 50-POUND DOG

Most dogs love fish, and you can be as creative as you want in making different variations on the same theme. The next four recipes follow a basic framework and include a fish, two vegetables, panko bread crumbs, and eggs. If your dog is highly sensitive to wheat, choose gluten-free bread crumbs instead. To complete the meal, I serve each fishcake with fresh, raw organ meat, a sprig of fresh parsley, and some cooked rice, millet, couscous, or quinoa.

2 pounds tuna steak

1 cup frozen or canned peas

1 medium sweet potato, diced

2 large eggs

2 cups panko bread crumbs

¾ cup uncooked brown rice

5 tablespoons chopped beef heart

5 sprigs fresh parsley, chopped

1 Preheat the oven to 375°F. Coat a large baking dish with nonstick cooking spray.

2 Pulse the tuna in a food processor to chop, then set it aside.

3 Cook the frozen peas according to the package directions and set them aside.

4 In a medium pot, cover the sweet potato with water and bring it to a boil. Cook it until it is soft when pierced with the tip of a knife about 20 minutes. Drain it and mash well in the pot. You should have about 1½ cups of mashed sweet potato.

5 In a large bowl, whisk together the eggs. Add the mashed sweet potato, the peas, tuna, and bread crumbs. Using your hands, mix all the ingredients well.

6 Make fishcakes that are approximately 3 inches in diameter (about 6 ounces each). Place them in the prepared baking dish and cover with foil. Bake for 25 minutes until golden brown. Remove them from the oven and let them cool for 15 minutes.

7 Meanwhile, prepare the rice as directed on the package. Set the cooked rice aside to cool. You should have about 1¼ cups of cooked rice.

8 To make one serving, refer to column 6 of the feeding chart on pages 34–35 and serve according to your dog's weight. Add ¼ cup of the rice, 1 tablespoon of chopped beef heart, and 1 sprig of chopped parsley to each fishcake (refer to columns 4 and 5 to adjust accordingly). Refrigerate leftovers in an airtight container for up to 3 days.

SWORDFISH SLIDERS
MAKES 5 SERVINGS FOR A 50-POUND DOG

Just as it is for humans, fish is an excellent source of essential fatty acids for dogs. If you want to make more than the recipe yields, you can double the recipe and then store the leftovers in the freezer for up to three months. I use zip-top storage bags to store the fishcakes in the freezer, which makes them easy to grab and defrost. Always remember to label and date the frozen meals.

2 pounds raw swordfish steak

1 cup diced yellow squash

2 large eggs

2 cups panko bread crumbs

½ cup mashed banana

½ cup (4 ounces) drained and chopped anchovies (flat fillets)

½ cup uncooked quinoa

5 tablespoons chopped beef heart

5 sprigs fresh parsley, chopped

1   Preheat the oven to 375°F. Coat a large baking dish with nonstick cooking spray.

2   Pulse the swordfish in a food processor to roughly chop it and set it aside.

3   Chop the squash in the food processor and set it aside. You should have about ½ cup of squash puree.

4   In a large bowl, whisk the eggs. Add the swordfish, squash puree, bread crumbs, banana, and anchovies. Using your hands, mix all the ingredients well.

5   Make fishcakes that are approximately 3 inches in diameter (about 6 ounces each). Place them in the prepared baking dish and cover with foil. Bake for 25 minutes, until golden brown. Remove and let cool for 15 minutes.

6   Meanwhile, prepare the quinoa as directed on the package. Set the cooked quinoa aside to cool. You should have about 1¼ cups of cooked quinoa.

7   To make one serving, refer to column 6 of the feeding chart on pages 34–35 and serve according to your dog's weight. Add ¼ cup of the quinoa, 1 tablespoon of the chopped beef heart, and 1 sprig of chopped parsley to each fishcake (refer to columns 4 and 5 to adjust accordingly). Refrigerate leftovers in an airtight container for up to 3 days.

SOULFUL FLOUNDER CAKES
MAKES 5 SERVINGS FOR A 50-POUND DOG

Since I live in an East Coast beach town, I can usually find a great variety of fish all year long at my local fish market. If you can't find flounder, you can substitute it with another light white fish such as tilapia.

¾ cup uncooked brown rice

2 pounds flounder fillet

2 cups chopped asparagus

2 large eggs

2 cups panko bread crumbs

½ cup canned pure pumpkin

¾ cup uncooked couscous

5 tablespoons chopped beef heart

5 sprigs fresh parsley, chopped

1 Preheat the oven to 375°F. Coat a large baking dish with nonstick cooking spray.

2 Prepare the rice as directed on the package. Set it aside to cool. You should have about 2 cups of cooked rice.

3 Pulse the flounder in a food processor to roughly chop it and set it aside.

4 Chop the asparagus in the food processor and set it aside. You should have 1 cup of chopped asparagus.

5 In a large bowl, whisk the eggs. Add the rice, flounder, bread crumbs, asparagus, and pumpkin. Using your hands, mix all the ingredients well.

6 Make fishcakes that are approximately 3 inches in diameter (about 6 ounces each). Place them in the prepared baking dish and cover with foil. Bake for 30 minutes, until golden brown. Remove and let cool for 15 minutes.

7 Meanwhile, prepare the couscous as directed on the package. Set aside to cool. You should have about 1¼ cups of cooked couscous.

8 To make one serving, refer to column 6 of the feeding chart on pages 34–35 and serve according to your dog's weight. Add ¼ cup of the couscous, 1 tablespoon of the chopped beef heart, and 1 sprig of chopped parsley to each fishcake serving (refer to columns 4 and 5 to adjust accordingly). Refrigerate any leftovers in an airtight container for up to 3 days.

MACKEREL AND PUMPKIN FLAPJACKS

MAKES 5 SERVINGS FOR A 50-POUND DOG

Jack mackerel is an oily fish rich in omega-3 fatty acids EPA and DHA, which makes it excellent for dogs—especially those with itchy or dry skin. The fish comes in cans and is either soaked in water or brine. Be sure to drain the fish fully before using it. The same goes for the artichoke hearts.

8 ounces canned unseasoned artichoke hearts, drained

2 large eggs

1½ cups canned pure pumpkin

4 (15-ounce) cans jack mackerel, drained

2 cups panko bread crumbs

½ cup uncooked millet

5 tablespoons chopped beef heart

5 sprigs fresh parsley, chopped

1 Preheat the oven to 375°F. Coat a large baking dish with nonstick cooking spray.

2 Chop the artichoke hearts in a food processor, and then set them aside. You should have about 1 cup of chopped artichoke hearts.

3 In a large bowl, whisk the eggs. Add the pumpkin, mackerel, bread crumbs, and artichoke hearts. Using your hands, mix all the ingredients well.

4 Make fishcakes that are approximately 3 inches in diameter (about 6 ounces each). Place them in the prepared baking dish, and cover with foil. Bake for 25 minutes, until golden brown. Remove them from the oven and let cool.

5 Prepare the millet as directed on the package. Set the cooked millet aside to cool. You should have about 1¼ cups of cooked millet.

6 To make one serving, refer to column 6 of the feeding chart on pages 34–35 and serve according to your dog's weight. Add ¼ cup of the millet, 1 tablespoon of the chopped beef heart, and 1 sprig's worth of chopped parsley to each fishcake serving (refer to columns 4 and 5 to adjust accordingly). Refrigerate leftovers in an airtight container for up to 3 days.

TOP-SHELF TURKEY BURGERS
MAKES 4 SERVINGS FOR A 50-POUND DOG

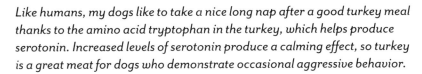

Like humans, my dogs like to take a nice long nap after a good turkey meal thanks to the amino acid tryptophan in the turkey, which helps produce serotonin. Increased levels of serotonin produce a calming effect, so turkey is a great meat for dogs who demonstrate occasional aggressive behavior.

4 medium red potatoes, diced	2 pounds ground turkey
1 cup chopped zucchini	½ cup mashed banana
2 large eggs	2 tablespoons minced beef heart

1 Preheat the oven to 375°F. Coat a large baking dish with nonstick cooking spray.

2 In a medium pot, cover the potatoes with water and bring it to a boil. Cook until the potatoes are soft when pierced with the tip of a knife, about 20 minutes. Drain them and mash well in the pot. You should have about 2½ cups of mashed potato.

3 Puree the zucchini in a food processor. You should have about ½ cup of zucchini puree.

4 In a large bowl, whisk the eggs. Add the turkey, zucchini, banana, mashed potatoes, and beef heart. Using your hands, mix all the ingredients well.

5 Make burgers that are approximately 3 inches in diameter (about 6 ounces each), place them in the prepared baking dish, and cover with foil. Bake for 30 to 40 minutes. Let the burgers cool completely before serving them.

6 To make one serving, refer to column 7 of the feeding chart on pages 34–35 and serve according to your dog's weight. Refrigerate leftovers in an airtight container for up to 3 days.

HEARTY HAMBURGERS
MAKES 4 SERVINGS FOR A 50-POUND DOG

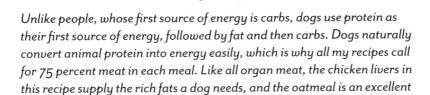

Unlike people, whose first source of energy is carbs, dogs use protein as their first source of energy, followed by fat and then carbs. Dogs naturally convert animal protein into energy easily, which is why all my recipes call for 75 percent meat in each meal. Like all organ meat, the chicken livers in this recipe supply the rich fats a dog needs, and the oatmeal is an excellent source of heart-healthy carbs.

1 ½ cups uncooked rolled oatmeal

1 ¼ cups chopped fresh green beans

2 large eggs

2 pounds ground beef

1 ½ cups panko bread crumbs

2 tablespoons minced chicken liver

1 Preheat the oven to 375°F.

2 Coat a large baking dish with nonstick cooking spray.

3 Prepare the oatmeal as directed on the package. Set it aside to cool. You should have about 2 cups of cooked oatmeal.

4 Puree the green beans in a food processor. You should have about 1 cup of green bean puree.

5 In a large bowl, whisk the eggs. Add the oatmeal, ground beef, green beans, bread crumbs, and chicken liver. Using your hands, mix all the ingredients well.

6 Make burgers that are approximately 3 inches in diameter (about 6 ounces each), place them in the prepared baking dish, and cover with foil. Bake them for 30 minutes. Let the burgers cool completely before serving them.

7 To make one serving, refer to column 7 of the feeding chart on pages 34–35 and serve according to your dog's weight. Refrigerate leftovers in an airtight container for up to 3 days.

CHARLIE'S CHICK BURGERS
MAKES 4 SERVINGS FOR A 50-POUND DOG

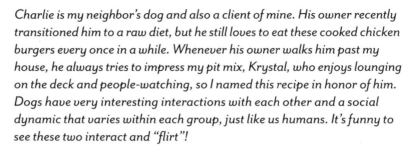

Charlie is my neighbor's dog and also a client of mine. His owner recently transitioned him to a raw diet, but he still loves to eat these cooked chicken burgers every once in a while. Whenever his owner walks him past my house, he always tries to impress my pit mix, Krystal, who enjoys lounging on the deck and people-watching, so I named this recipe in honor of him. Dogs have very interesting interactions with each other and a social dynamic that varies within each group, just like us humans. It's funny to see these two interact and "flirt"!

1¼ cups uncooked couscous

2 cups chopped celery

2 large eggs

2 pounds ground chicken

¼ cup canned pure pumpkin

2 tablespoons minced chicken liver

1 Preheat the oven to 350°F.

2 Coat a large baking dish with nonstick cooking spray.

3 Prepare the couscous as directed on the package. Set the cooked couscous aside to cool. You should have about 2½ cups of cooked couscous.

4 Puree the celery in a food processor. You should have about 1 cup of celery puree.

5 In a large bowl, whisk the eggs. Add the chicken, couscous, pureed celery, pumpkin, and chicken liver. Using your hands, mix all the ingredients well.

6 Make burgers that are approximately 3 inches in diameter (about 6 ounces each), place them in the prepared baking dish, and cover with foil. Bake them for 35 to 40 minutes. Let them cool completely before serving.

7 To make one serving, refer to column 7 of the feeding chart on pages 34–35 and serve according to your dog's weight. Refrigerate leftovers in an airtight container for up to 3 days.

PRETTY EASY PORK BURGERS

MAKES 4 SERVINGS FOR A 50-POUND DOG

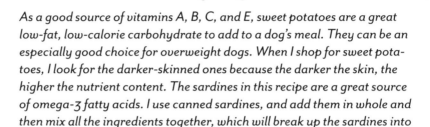

As a good source of vitamins A, B, C, and E, sweet potatoes are a great low-fat, low-calorie carbohydrate to add to a dog's meal. They can be an especially good choice for overweight dogs. When I shop for sweet pota-toes, I look for the darker-skinned ones because the darker the skin, the higher the nutrient content. The sardines in this recipe are a great source of omega-3 fatty acids. I use canned sardines, and add them in whole and then mix all the ingredients together, which will break up the sardines into more bite-size pieces.

1 small sweet potato, diced	2 pounds ground pork
¾ cup uncooked brown rice	⅓ cup (3 ounces) sardines, drained
2 large eggs	2 tablespoons minced beef heart

1 Preheat the oven to 350°F.

2 Coat a large baking dish with nonstick cooking spray.

3 In a medium pot, cover the potato pieces with water and bring it to a boil. Cook until the potatoes are soft when pierced with the tip of a knife, about 25 minutes. Drain them and mash well in the pot. You should have about 1 cup of mashed sweet potato.

4 Prepare the rice as directed on the package. Set the cooked rice aside to cool. You should have about 2 cups of cooked rice.

5 In a large bowl, whisk the eggs. Add the pork, rice, mashed potatoes, sardines, and beef heart. Using your hands, mix all the ingredients well.

6 Make burgers that are approximately 3 inches in diameter (about 6 ounces each), place them in the prepared baking dish, and cover with foil. Bake them for 35 to 40 minutes. Let them cool completely before serving them.

7 To make one serving, refer to column 7 of the feeding chart on pages 34–35 and serve according to your dog's weight. Refrigerate leftovers in an airtight container for up to 3 days.

BAD TO THE BONE STEW
MAKES 5 TO 6 SERVINGS FOR A 50-POUND DOG

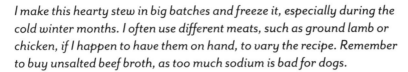

I make this hearty stew in big batches and freeze it, especially during the cold winter months. I often use different meats, such as ground lamb or chicken, if I happen to have them on hand, to vary the recipe. Remember to buy unsalted beef broth, as too much sodium is bad for dogs.

2 tablespoons butter

2½ pounds boneless beef chuck

10 small red potatoes, quartered

1 pound peeled, cubed butternut squash

1 quart unsalted beef broth

1 cup mashed banana

3 tablespoons cornstarch

1 In a large sauté pan, melt the butter over medium-low heat. Add the beef and cook until it is browned. Remove the meat from the pan and set it aside.

2 To the same pan, add the potatoes and butternut squash. Sauté them for 5 minutes and remove them from the heat.

3 In a large stock pot, combine the browned meat, squash, potatoes, broth, and banana. Cook over medium heat, covered, for 20 minutes.

4 In a separate bowl, mix the cornstarch with 1 tablespoon of water and stir until smooth. Add the cornstarch to the pot and stir slowly for 2 minutes to incorporate.

5 Cover the pot and cook the stew for 25 minutes. Let the stew cool completely before serving.

6 To make one serving, refer to column 1 of the feeding chart on pages 34–35 and measure in cups according to your dog's weight. Refrigerate leftovers in an airtight container for up to 3 days.

MEATLOAF MONDAY
MAKES 4 SERVINGS FOR A 50-POUND DOG

Even dogs can get a case of the Monday blues every once in a while! This recipe is chock-full of vitamin-rich ingredients that will give your dog a nice boost of energy to start the week off right. You can easily substitute any other type of meat you have on hand to vary the recipe.

½ cup chopped broccoli

½ cup uncooked quinoa pasta

2 large eggs

2 pounds ground beef

½ cup unsweetened shredded coconut

4 tablepoons fish oil

4 tablespoons apple cider vinegar

1 Preheat the oven to 375°F. Coat a 9-by-5-inch loaf pan with nonstick cooking spray.

2 Over simmering water, steam the broccoli for 3 minutes. Drain, then puree it in a food processor. You should have about ½ cup of broccoli puree.

3 Prepare the pasta as directed on the package. Set the cooked pasta aside to cool. When cool, puree it in a food processor with a little water, if needed. You should have about 1 cup of pureed pasta.

4 In a large bowl, whisk the eggs. Add the beef, pureed pasta, and broccoli. Using your hands, mix all the ingredients well. Press the meatloaf mixture into the prepared loaf pan. Sprinkle the coconut evenly on top.

5 Bake the meatloaf for 45 minutes, or until the top is browned. Let it cool for 30 minutes before serving.

6 To make one serving, refer to column 1 of the feeding chart on pages 34–35 and measure in cups according to your dog's weight. Add 1 tablespoon of the fish oil and 1 tablespoon of the vinegar to each serving (refer to column 9 to adjust accordingly). Refrigerate any leftovers in an airtight container for up to 3 days.

TACO TUESDAY

MAKES 4 SERVINGS FOR A 50-POUND DOG

In this recipe, I use stone-ground yellow corn taco shells, but you can also use a whole wheat pita. A small amount of corn grains—where the whole kernel is ground down into dough—is perfectly fine to give your dog; it's when a dog's diet is composed mostly of fillers and by-products that his health can become compromised. If your dog finds eating the taco shell or pita whole challenging, break it up in his bowl.

1 tablespoon olive oil

2 pounds ground turkey

1 cup chopped celery

8 stone-ground yellow corn taco shells

½ cup plain Greek yogurt

¼ cup minced chicken liver

½ cup shredded low-fat mozzarella cheese

1   In a large sauté pan, heat the oil over medium-low heat. Add the turkey and cook until it is browned. Drain off any excess fat and set the meat aside to cool.

2   Puree the celery in a food processor. You should have about ½ cup of celery puree.

3   Fill each taco shell with ½ cup of the turkey, 1 tablespoon of the pureed celery, 1 tablespoon of the yogurt, ½ tablespoon of the liver, and 1 tablespoon of the cheese.

4   To make one serving, refer to column 1 of the feeding chart on pages 34–35 and measure in cups according to your dog's weight. Refrigerate any leftovers in an airtight container for up to 3 days.

WIENER SCHNITZEL WEDNESDAY

MAKES 4 SERVINGS FOR A 50-POUND DOG

─────⟨ ⬭ ⟩─────

Whenever I make this recipe, I go to my butcher and ask him for 2 pounds of pork cutlets pounded thin. You can also use chicken or turkey cutlets as a substitution. If I'm short on time, I buy packaged precooked beets and just puree them in a food processor. However, if you have the time to make fresh beets, that is always best. Beets are a good source of magnesium, potassium, and vitamins A and C and can typically be found year-round in most grocery stores.

1 small red beet	8 large eggs
1 small sweet potato, diced	2 cups amaranth flour
¾ cup uncooked brown rice	2 pounds chicken or pork cutlets pounded to ¼ inch thick

1 Preheat the oven to 450°F.

2 Coat two large baking dishes with nonstick cooking spray.

3 If you are using a fresh beet, boil it for about 45 minutes, until tender when pierced with the tip of a knife. Drain it and set aside to cool for 30 minutes. When the beet is fully cooled, peel it and then puree it in a food processor. You should have about ½ cup of beet puree.

4 Put the sweet potatoes in one of the baking dishes. Bake them for 1 hour, or until they are soft when pierced with the tip of a knife. (Leave the oven on.) Set them aside to cool, then mash them. You should have about ½ cup of mashed sweet potato.

5 Reduce the oven temperature to 325°F.

6 Prepare the rice as directed on the package. Set it aside to cool. You should have about 2 cups of cooked rice.

7 Hard-boil 4 of the eggs as directed on page 24.

8 In a shallow bowl, whisk the remaining 4 eggs. Pour the flour into a separate shallow bowl.

9 Dip each cutlet in the egg and then in the flour and place them in the remaining prepared baking dish. Bake them for 20 minutes, or until golden brown. Set them aside to cool, then chop the cutlets into bite-size pieces.

10 To make one serving, combine 1 cup chopped cutlet, 1 tablespoon of the beet puree, 1 tablespoon of the mashed sweet potato, ¼ cup of the rice, and 1 hard-boiled egg (shell on), sliced into quarters, in your dog's bowl. Refer to refer to columns 2, 3, 4, and 8 of the feeding chart on pages 34–35 to adjust according to your dog's weight. Refrigerate any leftovers in an airtight container for up to 3 days.

THURSDAY THANKSGIVING
MAKES 4 SERVINGS FOR A 50-POUND DOG

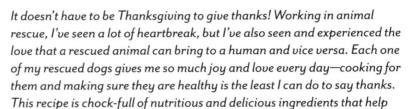

It doesn't have to be Thanksgiving to give thanks! Working in animal rescue, I've seen a lot of heartbreak, but I've also seen and experienced the love that a rescued animal can bring to a human and vice versa. Each one of my rescued dogs gives me so much joy and love every day—cooking for them and making sure they are healthy is the least I can do to say thanks. This recipe is chock-full of nutritious and delicious ingredients that help keep your beloved pup healthy and happy.

2 tablespoons olive oil

2½ pounds ground turkey

⅓ cup uncooked barley

1 garlic clove, minced

1 cup chopped fresh spinach

¼ cup (2 ounces) minced beef heart

¼ cup canned pure pumpkin

¼ cup salmon oil

4 sprigs fresh parsley, chopped

1 In a large sauté pan, heat 1 tablespoon of the olive oil over medium-low heat. Add the turkey and cook until it is browned. Drain any excess fat and set the turkey aside to cool.

2 Prepare the barley as directed on the package. Set it aside to cool. You should have about 1 cup of cooked barley.

3 In a large sauté pan, heat the remaining 1 tablespoon of olive oil over medium-low heat. Add the garlic and sauté until it is lightly browned, about 3 minutes. Add the spinach and sauté, stirring frequently, until wilted, about 5 minutes. Remove the pan from the heat and let cool.

4 Once cooled, puree the spinach and garlic mixture in a food processor and set it aside. You should have about ¼ cup of spinach-garlic puree.

TO MAKE ONE SERVING

1⅓ cups cooked ground turkey

¼ cup cooked barley

1 tablespoon spinach-garlic puree

1 tablespoon minced beef heart

1 tablespoon canned pumpkin

1 tablespoon salmon oil

1 sprig chopped fresh parsley

In your dog's bowl, combine the turkey, barley, spinach-garlic puree, beef heart, pumpkin, salmon oil, and parsley. Refer to refer to columns 2, 3, 4, 5, and 9 of the feeding chart on pages 34–35 to adjust according to your dog's weight. Refrigerate any leftovers in an airtight container for up to 3 days.

FRIDAY PLAYDATE PIZZA
MAKES 4 SERVINGS FOR A 50-POUND DOG

Every Friday evening during the summer, I have a tradition at my house. I invite my friends and family over for pizza and wine on the porch, to watch the sunset and enjoy the nice summer evening. Over the years, this has also become a great opportunity to get all our dogs together. Since I love making my own pizza, I came up with this easy dog-friendly recipe so the dogs could join in the Friday night fun too. The pizza comes out best if you have a pizza stone because it allows the crust to cook evenly, but if you don't have one you can use a baking sheet and your dog probably won't complain. If you use a pizza stone, don't preheat it—you will be spreading the grits directly on the stone.

1 cup uncooked grits

1 pound ground beef

8 ounces canned unseasoned artichoke hearts, drained and chopped

½ cup shredded part-skim mozzarella cheese

1 Preheat the oven to 450°F. Coat a pizza stone or baking sheet with nonstick cooking spray.

2 Prepare the grits according to the package directions. Set them aside to cool for about 20 minutes. You should have about 2 cups of cooked grits.

3 Using a spatula, evenly spread the cooked grits onto the greased pizza stone or baking sheet. Evenly spread the beef on top of the grits to make the second layer. Next, add the artichoke hearts, and top with the cheese.

4 Bake the pizza for 10 to 12 minutes, until the meat is browned. Remove from the oven and let it cool for 30 minutes.

5 Chop the pizza into bite-size pieces. To make one serving, refer to column 1 of the feeding chart on pages 34–35 and measure in cups according to your dog's weight. Refrigerate any leftovers in an airtight container for up to 3 days.

CHAPTER 3

RAW RECIPES

THE RAW FOOD DIET FOR DOGS—also referred to as the Bones and Raw Food diet (BARF)—is becoming increasingly popular in the dog world right now, as owners have begun to see the amazing health benefits it offers. There are several controversial points and myths surrounding the raw food diet that should be addressed here.

The controversy over the raw food diet for dogs is similar to the raw milk trend that's very big right now among us humans! The FDA's fight to maintain the illegal status of raw milk is very similar to many traditional veterinarians' fight to maintain the thinking that feeding a raw food diet is dangerous. The truth is, both offer amazing health benefits. In many cases, I've seen dogs cured from cancer and other serious illness after their owners transitioned them to a raw food diet. Many non-holistic vets would be put out of business if all the dogs they treated were on a raw food diet! And think of how many pet food companies would be out of business if the American Veterinary Medical Association condoned either the raw food diet or homemade cooked diets for dogs—or both!

One of the main arguments against the raw food diet is the risk of *E. coli* and *salmonella*. The most important thing about feeding a raw diet is properly sourcing the meat and being aware of the quality and freshness of the raw meat you feed your dog. Raw meat is biologically appropriate for your dog. With their short, acidic digestive tract, dogs are biologically engineered to eat raw meat. Their teeth are designed to rip and tear flesh and crunch bone. Being smart about the meat you use is the best precaution to take. Here are some pointers to ensure that raw meat is safe:

Find a reputable butcher or meat supplier. There are many butchers who sell meat specifically for dogs. Reputable butchers get their meat from reputable suppliers, and although you may have to pay a bit more for good, organic meat, it's very worth it.

If you cannot find a supplier or butcher, find a holistic vet in your area. Many holistic vets who recommend homemade meals either sell meat at their office or can direct you to a reputable supplier in your area.

Be aware of expiration dates. Common sense says that you should not purchase meat that's nearing its expiration date, especially if you plan to use the meat raw.

Be aware of smell. It's pretty easy to tell when meat starts to go bad. Even if meat hasn't passed its expiration date, smell it to be sure before giving it to your dog. It should smell fresh, with no sour or strong odors. Bad meat has a very unpleasant smell.

Never feed your pet raw fish. Raw fish is extremely dangerous for dogs because many types of fish, such as salmon and trout, contain bacteria and dangerous parasites that can lead to serious illness. Although I advocate feeding raw meat, I never feed a dog raw fish.

If you decide to put your dog on a raw diet, I recommend a four-week transition period. The transition schedule provided in this book provides a basic outline for a healthy, average-size dog that gets regular exercise. Please note that serving sizes in the chart are not specific for any one particular dog, but rather provide a ratio guideline. My transition diet moves a dog from commercial dog food to home-cooked food and finally to a raw diet. Once you fully transition to raw food by week four, you can still feed cooked food also. The goal here is to get your dog's system ready for a home-cooked diet, a raw diet, or a combination of both.

Always use your best judgment when adjusting serving sizes, as each dog is different and should be treated as an individual. I always tell my clients to use their judgment when it comes to their pet's care because they know their dog better than anyone else.

The recipes and serving sizes in this chapter are for a fifty-pound dog. Use the feeding chart on pages 34–35 or the bookmark in the front of this book to adjust serving sizes based on your dog's weight. The recipes generally call for enough ingredients to make four servings for a fifty-pound dog. It's important to store ingredients in these recipes in the refrigerator in separate airtight containers, and then mix them together into a single serving at each meal. This ensures you can monitor the freshness of individual ingredients, especially organ meat, which tends to have a shorter shelf life than the rest of the ingredients. Additionally, you may find you have every ingredient except one or you don't have enough of one. Storing ingredients separately allows you to make substitutions; just remember to keep the measurements the same when you're mixing the recipe. As a reminder, never serve food that's more than three days old. You may need to adjust the amount you make and store accordingly.

WEEK ONE TRANSITION CHART

	DAY 1	DAY 2	DAY 3	DAY 4	DAY 5	DAY 6	DAY 7
BREAKFAST	½ cup cooked beef ½ cup dry food ¼ cup brown rice 1 tablespoon chopped sardines	½ cup cooked beef ½ cup dry food ¼ cup brown rice 1 tablespoon chopped sardines	½ cup cooked beef ½ cup dry food ¼ cup brown rice 1 tablespoon chopped sardines	½ cup cooked ground turkey ½ cup dry food ¼ cup oatmeal 1 tablespoon chopped sardines	½ cup cooked ground turkey ½ cup dry food ¼ cup oatmeal 1 tablespoon chopped sardines	½ cup cooked ground turkey ½ cup dry food ¼ cup oatmeal 1 tablespoon chopped sardines	½ cup cooked ground turkey ½ cup dry food ¼ cup oatmeal 1 tablespoon chopped sardines
SNACK	1 Pumpkin Spice Treat (see page 113), hard-boiled egg	½ raw turkey neck (frozen) or 2 raw chicken wings (frozen)	1 Pumpkin Spice Treat (see page 113), hard-boiled egg	½ raw turkey neck (frozen) or 2 raw chicken wings (frozen)	1 Veggie Oatmeal Bite (see page 119), hard-boiled egg	½ raw turkey neck (frozen) or 2 raw chicken wings (frozen)	1 Veggie Oatmeal Bite (see page 119), hard-boiled egg
DINNER	½ cup cooked beef ½ cup dry food ⅓ cup brown rice 1 tablespoon pumpkin	½ cup cooked beef ½ cup dry food ⅓ cup brown rice 1 tablespoon pumpkin	½ cup cooked beef ½ cup dry food ⅓ cup brown rice 1 tablespoon pumpkin	½ cup cooked ground turkey ½ cup dry food ⅓ cup oatmeal 1 tablespoon pumpkin	½ cup cooked ground turkey ½ cup dry food ⅓ cup oatmeal 1 tablespoon pumpkin	½ cup cooked ground turkey ½ cup dry food ⅓ cup oatmeal 1 tablespoon pumpkin	½ cup cooked ground turkey ½ cup dry food ⅓ cup oatmeal 1 tablespoon pumpkin
EXTRAS	1 tablespoon apple cider vinegar, 1 sprig of parsley	1 tablespoon apple cider vinegar, 1 sprig of parsley	1 tablespoon apple cider vinegar, 1 sprig of parsley	1 tablespoon apple cider vinegar, 1 sprig of parsley	1 tablespoon apple cider vinegar, 1 sprig of parsley	1 tablespoon apple cider vinegar, 1 sprig of parsley	1 tablespoon apple cider vinegar, 1 sprig of parsley

LET'S REVIEW

The goal of this week is to get your dog used to some cooked meat, in particular beef and turkey. Since I recommend feeding twice a day with a snack mid-day, you will see I keep things fairly consistent. Days 1 to 3 include cooked beef and brown rice as the main components of the meal, but you are still also feeding some commercial pet food. I add pumpkin in right away because it helps alleviate some of the digestive issues that might occur as you change your dog's diet. Days 4 to 7 include cooked ground turkey and oatmeal. I keep the meat and source of carbohydrates the same for both breakfast and dinner intentionally. Not only does it save you time, but it also gives your dog time to adjust to the new food. I don't like to add too many different foods to Week 1. Keep it simple! Extras should be added to one meal a day.

WEEK TWO TRANSITION CHART

	DAY 1	DAY 2	DAY 3	DAY 4	DAY 5	DAY 6	DAY 7
BREAKFAST	1 cup cooked ground beef 1 tablespoon mashed sweet potato ¼ cup couscous	1 cup cooked ground beef 1 tablespoon mashed sweet potato ¼ cup couscous	1 cup cooked ground beef 1 tablespoon mashed sweet potato ¼ cup couscous	1 cup cooked ground chicken 1 tablespoon cooked pureed peas ¼ cup quinoa	1 cup cooked ground chicken 1 tablespoon cooked pureed peas ¼ cup quinoa	1 cup cooked ground chicken 1 tablespoon cooked pureed peas ¼ cup quinoa	1 cup cooked ground chicken 1 tablespoon cooked pureed peas ¼ cup quinoa
SNACK	1 Sardine and Oatmeal Tart (see page 117), hard boiled egg, 1 marrow bone	½ raw turkey neck (frozen) or 2 raw chicken wings (frozen)	1 Sardine and Oatmeal Tart (see page 117), hard boiled egg, 1 marrow bone	½ raw turkey neck (frozen) or 2 raw chicken wings (frozen)	1 Thanksgiving Bite (see page 132), hard boiled egg, 1 marrow bone	½ raw turkey neck (frozen) or 2 raw chicken wings (frozen)	1 Thanksgiving Bite (see page 132), hard boiled egg, 1 marrow bone
DINNER	½ cup raw ground beef ½ cup dry food ⅓ cup couscous 2 tablespoons pumpkin	½ cup raw ground beef ½ cup dry food ⅓ cup couscous 2 tablespoons pumpkin	½ cup raw ground beef ½ cup dry food ⅓ cup couscous 2 tablespoons pumpkin	½ cup raw ground chicken ½ cup dry food ⅓ cup quinoa 2 tablespoons pumpkin	½ cup raw ground chicken ½ cup dry food ⅓ cup quinoa 2 tablespoons pumpkin	½ cup raw ground chicken ½ cup dry food ⅓ cup quinoa 2 tablespoons pumpkin	½ cup raw ground chicken ½ cup dry food ⅓ cup quinoa 2 tablespoons pumpkin
EXTRAS	1 tablespoon apple cider vinegar	1 tablespoon apple cider vinegar	1 tablespoon apple cider vinegar	1 tablespoon apple cider vinegar	1 tablespoon apple cider vinegar	1 tablespoon apple cider vinegar	1 tablespoon apple cider vinegar

LET'S REVIEW

During Week 2 there are three important changes: First, I am only serving commercial pet food for one meal. Second, I am introducing raw meat at dinner time and third, I'm adding in cooked vegetables in one meal. Cooked vegetables are a little easier on the digestive system, which is why I serve only cooked, and not raw veggies, for Week 2. I introduced raw bones including turkey necks, chicken wings and sections, and marrow bones in Week 1 as they are an important part of the raw food diet. You can often get these right from the butcher or in the frozen food section of your local grocery store. Feeding raw bones frozen is a lot less messy.

WEEK THREE TRANSITION CHART

	DAY 1	DAY 2	DAY 3	DAY 4	DAY 5	DAY 6	DAY 7
BREAKFAST	1 cup raw ground lamb 1 tablespoon pureed beets ¼ cup red quinoa	1 cup raw ground lamb 1 tablespoon pureed beets ¼ cup red quinoa	1 cup raw ground lamb 1 tablespoon pureed beets ¼ cup red quinoa	1 cup raw ground turkey 1 tablespoon pureed zucchini ¼ cup oatmeal 1 tablespoon yogurt	1 cup raw ground turkey 1 tablespoon pureed zucchini ¼ cup oatmeal 1 tablespoon yogurt	1 cup raw ground turkey 1 tablespoon pureed zucchini ¼ cup oatmeal 1 tablespoon yogurt	1 cup raw ground turkey 1 tablespoon pureed zucchini ¼ cup oatmeal 1 tablespoon yogurt
SNACK	Marrow bone	KONG stuffed with Pork Loin Pâté (see page 137)	Marrow bone	KONG stuffed with Chicken and Cheese Pâté (see page 137)	Marrow bone	KONG stuffed with Bella's Beef Bites (see page 128)	Marrow bone
DINNER	1 16-oz. can sardines 1 tablespoon pureed celery ⅓ cup millet 1 teaspoon beef heart	1 16-oz. can sardines 1 tablespoon pureed celery ⅓ cup millet 1 teaspoon beef heart	1 16-oz. can sardines 1 tablespoon pureed celery ⅓ cup millet 1 teaspoon beef heart	1 16-oz. can Mackerel 1 tablespoon steamed kale ⅓ cup brown rice 1 teaspoon beef heart	1 16-oz. can Mackerel 1 tablespoon steamed kale ⅓ cup brown rice 1 teaspoon beef heart	1 16-oz. can Mackerel 1 tablespoon steamed kale ⅓ cup brown rice 1 teaspoon beef heart	1 16-oz. can Mackerel 1 tablespoon steamed kale ⅓ cup brown rice 1 teaspoon beef heart
EXTRAS	1 tablespoon apple cider vinegar, 1 garlic clove, minced	1 tablespoon apple cider vinegar	1 tablespoon apple cider vinegar, 1 garlic clove, minced	1 tablespoon apple cider vinegar, 1 teaspoon flaxseed oil	1 tablespoon apple cider vinegar, 1 garlic clove, minced	1 tablespoon apple cider vinegar	1 tablespoon apple cider vinegar, 1 garlic clove, minced

LET'S REVIEW	During Week 3, I no longer serve commercial pet food and I introduce raw vegetables. Use your own discretion as to whether or not your dog is ready for these next steps. If he appears to be tolerating the transition well, then move on to Week 3. If you feel he's not ready, you can always repeat Week 2. Week 3 is when I introduce canned fish as a meal, and organ meat. Fish is a great source of essential fatty acids, which support heart, joint, skin, and hair health. I also recommend introducing garlic in a few meals a week at this stage, but in very small amounts.

WEEK FOUR TRANSITION CHART

	DAY 1	DAY 2	DAY 3	DAY 4	DAY 5	DAY 6	DAY 7
BREAKFAST	5 raw chicken wings (frozen)	3 raw turkey necks (frozen)	5 raw chicken wings (frozen)	3 raw turkey necks (frozen)	5 raw chicken wings (frozen)	3 raw turkey necks (frozen)	5 raw chicken wings (frozen)
SNACK	Marrow bone	1 Camper's Campfire Treat (see page 127)	Marrow bone	1 Cesar's Favorite Chicken Liver Treat (see page 114)	Marrow bone	1 Pork Loin Fritter (see page 116)	Marrow bone
DINNER	1 cup raw meat 1 tablespoon raw vegetable ¼ cup brown rice 1 teaspoon beef heart ½ hard-boiled egg	1 cup raw meat 1 tablespoon raw vegetable ¼ cup brown rice 1 teaspoon beef heart ½ hard-boiled egg	1 cup raw meat 1 tablespoon raw vegetable ¼ cup brown rice 1 teaspoon beef heart ½ hard-boiled egg	1 cup raw meat 1 tablespoon raw vegetable ¼ cup quinoa 1 teaspoon beef heart ½ hard-boiled egg	1 cup raw meat 1 tablespoon raw vegetable ¼ cup quinoa 1 teaspoon beef heart ½ hard-boiled egg	1 cup raw meat 1 tablespoon raw vegetable ¼ cup quinoa 1 teaspoon beef heart ½ hard-boiled egg	1 cup raw meat 1 tablespoon raw vegetable ¼ cup quinoa 1 teaspoon beef heart ½ hard-boiled egg
EXTRAS	1 tablespoon apple cider vinegar, 1 teaspoon flaxseed oil	1 tablespoon apple cider vinegar, 1 teaspoon coconut oil	1 tablespoon apple cider vinegar, 1 garlic clove minced	1 tablespoon apple cider vinegar, 1 teaspoon flaxseed oil	1 tablespoon apple cider vinegar, 1 garlic clove minced, 1 teaspoon coconut oil	1 tablespoon apple cider vinegar, 1 teaspoon flaxseed oil	1 tablespoon apple cider vinegar, 1 teaspoon coconut oil

LET'S REVIEW

By Week 4, raw bones can make up an entire meal. As a general rule of thumb, a 50-pound dog should get about 5 wings, or 2 turkey necks, as a meal. Never feed a cooked bone because cooking the bones changes their composition, and they might splinter and injure your dog. As a precaution, I never leave my dogs unattended while they have raw bones. An uncooked bone is rarely a choking hazard, but it's always best to supervise your dog when you give her a bone or any toy.

BEEF, QUINOA, AND SWEET POTATOES

MAKES 4 SERVINGS FOR A 50-POUND DOG

¾ cup uncooked quinoa

1 small sweet potato, diced

2 pounds ground beef

¼ cup (2 ounces) chicken liver, chopped

4 teaspoons chopped fresh parsley

¼ cup canned pure pumpkin

1 Prepare the quinoa as directed on the package. Set it aside to cool. You should have about 2 cups of cooked quinoa.

2 In a small pot, cover the sweet potato with water and bring it to a boil. Cook it until it is soft when pierced with the tip of a knife. Drain the potato and mash it well in the pot. You should have about 1 cup of mashed sweet potato.

TO MAKE ONE SERVING

1⅓ cups raw ground beef

½ cup cooked quinoa

¼ cup mashed sweet potato

1 tablespoon chopped chicken liver

1 teaspoon chopped fresh parsley

1 tablespoon canned pumpkin

In your dog's bowl, combine the beef, quinoa, sweet potato, chicken liver, parsley, and pumpkin. Refer to the feeding chart on pages 34–35, columns 2, 3, 4, 5, and 9, and adjust according to your dog's weight. Mix well to combine. Refrigerate any leftovers in an airtight container for up to 3 days.

BEEF, ZUCCHINI, AND COUSCOUS

MAKES 4 SERVINGS FOR A 50-POUND DOG

1 cup uncooked couscous

½ cup chopped zucchini

2 pounds ground beef

¼ cup (2 ounces) chopped beef heart

4 hard-boiled eggs (see page 24)

¼ cup plain yogurt

1 Prepare the couscous as directed on the package. Set it aside to cool. You should have about 2 cups of cooked couscous.

2 Puree the zucchini in a food processor. You should have about ¼ cup of zucchini puree.

TO MAKE ONE SERVING

1⅓ cups raw ground beef

½ cup cooked couscous

1 tablespoon pureed zucchini

1 tablespoon beef heart

1 hard-boiled egg (shell on), cut in half or smaller pieces

1 tablespoon plain yogurt

In your dog's bowl, combine the beef, couscous, zucchini, beef heart, egg, and yogurt. Refer to the feeding chart on pages 34–35, columns 2, 3, 4, 5, 8, and 9, and adjust according to your dog's weight. Mix well to combine. Refrigerate any leftovers in an airtight container for up to 3 days.

BEEF, POTATOES, AND CARROTS

MAKES 4 SERVINGS FOR A 50-POUND DOG

2 cups diced potatoes

¼ cup chopped carrots

2 pounds ground beef

¼ cup (2 ounces) chicken gizzard, chopped

¼ cup (2 ounces) drained and chopped sardines

¼ cup flaxseed meal

1. In a medium pot, cover the potatoes with water and bring to a boil. Cook it until they are soft when pierced with the tip of a knife. Drain the potatoes and set aside to cool.

2. Puree the carrot in a food processor. You should have about ¼ cup of carrot puree.

TO MAKE ONE SERVING

1⅓ cups raw ground beef

½ cup cooked potatoes

1 tablespoon pureed carrot

1 tablespoon raw chicken gizzard

1 tablespoon sardines

1 tablespoon flaxseed meal

In your dog's bowl, combine the beef, potatoes, carrot, gizzard, sardines, and flaxseed meal. Refer to the feeding chart on pages 34–35, columns 2, 3, 4, 5, and 9, and adjust according to your dog's weight. Mix well to combine. Refrigerate any leftovers in an airtight container for up to 3 days.

BEEF, MILLET, AND KALE

MAKES 4 SERVINGS FOR A 50-POUND DOG

¾ cup uncooked millet

½ cup chopped kale

2 pounds ground beef

¼ cup (2 ounces) canned jack mackerel, drained

¼ cup canned pure pumpkin

1 Prepare the millet as directed on the package. Set it aside to cool. You should have about 2 cups of cooked millet.

2 Fill a large saucepan with 1 inch of water and place a vegetable steamer inside the pan. Place the kale in the steamer. Bring the water to a boil and steam the kale until bright green and wilted. Remove the steamer basket. Place the kale in a bowl and set aside to cool. You should have about ¼ cup of steamed kale.

TO MAKE ONE SERVING

1⅓ cups raw ground beef

½ cup cooked millet

1 tablespoon steamed kale

1 tablespoon jack mackerel

1 tablespoon canned pumpkin

In your dog's bowl, combine the beef, millet, kale, mackerel, and pumpkin. Refer to the feeding chart on pages 34–35, columns 2, 3, 4, and 9, and adjust according to your dog's weight. Mix well to combine. Refrigerate any leftovers in an airtight container for up to 3 days.

LAMB, BROWN RICE, AND BEETS

MAKES 4 SERVINGS FOR A 50-POUND DOG

¾ cup uncooked brown rice

1 small beet

2 pounds ground lamb

¼ cup wheat germ

4 teaspoons chopped fresh parsley

¼ cup plain yogurt

1 Prepare the rice as directed on the package. Set it aside to cool. You should have about 2 cups of cooked rice.

2 Place the beet in a small saucepan with enough water to cover. Bring the water to a boil and cook for about 45 minutes, or until the beet is tender. Set aside to cool. Peel the cooled beet and puree in a food processor. You should have about ¼ cup of beet puree.

TO MAKE ONE SERVING

1⅓ cups raw ground lamb

½ cup cooked brown rice

1 tablespoon pureed beet

1 tablespoon wheat germ

1 tablespoon plain yogurt

1 teaspoon chopped fresh parsley

In your dog's bowl, combine the lamb, rice, beets, wheat germ, yogurt, and parsley. Refer to the feeding chart on pages 34–35, columns 2, 3, 4, and 9, and adjust according to your dog's weight. Mix well to combine. Refrigerate any leftovers in an airtight container for up to 3 days.

LAMB, QUINOA PASTA, AND SQUASH

MAKES 4 SERVINGS FOR A 50-POUND DOG

1 cup uncooked quinoa pasta

½ cup chopped yellow squash

2 pounds ground lamb

¼ cup (2 ounces) chopped beef heart

4 hard-boiled eggs, shell on
(see page 24)

1 Prepare the pasta as directed on the package. Set it aside to cool. Chop it into smaller pieces and set aside. You should have about 2 cups of cooked pasta.

2 Puree the squash in a food processor. You should have about ¼ cup of squash puree.

TO MAKE ONE SERVING

1⅓ cups raw ground lamb

½ cup cooked quinoa pasta

1 tablespoon pureed yellow squash

1 tablespoon raw beef heart

1 hard-boiled egg (shell on), cut in
half or smaller pieces

In your dog's bowl, combine the lamb, pasta, squash, beef heart, and egg. Refer to the feeding chart on pages 34–35, columns 2, 3, 4, 5, and 8, and adjust according to your dog's weight. Mix well to combine. Refrigerate any leftovers in an airtight container for up to 3 days.

LAMB, SWEET POTATO, AND FLAXSEED

MAKES 4 SERVINGS FOR A 50-POUND DOG

1 large sweet potato, diced

¼ cup chopped carrots

2 pounds ground lamb

¼ cup (2 ounces) chicken gizzard, chopped

¼ cup flaxseed meal

1 In a medium pot, cover the potatoes with water and bring to a boil. Cook until the potatoes are soft when pierced with the tip of a knife. Drain them and mash well in the pot. You should have about 2 cups of mashed sweet potato.

2 Puree the carrot in a food processor. You should have about ¼ cup of carrot puree.

TO MAKE ONE SERVING

1⅓ cups raw ground lamb

½ cup mashed sweet potato

1 tablepoon pureed carrot

1 tablespoon raw chicken gizzard

1 tablespoon flaxseed meal

In your dog's bowl, combine the lamb, potato, carrot, gizzard, and flaxseed meal. Refer to the feeding chart on pages 34–35, columns 2, 3, 4, 5, and 9, and adjust according to your dog's weight. Mix well to combine. Refrigerate any leftovers in an airtight container for up to 3 days.

LAMB, MILLET, AND BANANA
MAKES 4 SERVINGS FOR A 50-POUND DOG

¾ cup uncooked millet

½ cup chopped celery

2 pounds ground lamb

¼ cup mashed banana

¼ cup (2 ounces) sardines, drained

¼ cup flaxseed meal

1 Prepare the millet as directed on the package. Set it aside to cool. You should have about 2 cups of cooked millet.

2 Puree the celery in a food processor. You should have about 1 cup of celery puree.

TO MAKE ONE SERVING

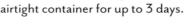

1⅓ cups raw ground lamb

½ cup cooked millet

1 tablespoon pureed celery

1 tablespoon mashed banana

1 tablespoon sardines

1 tablespoon flaxseed meal

In your dog's bowl, combine the lamb, millet, celery, banana, sardines, and flaxseed meal. Refer to the feeding chart on pages 34–35, columns 2, 3, 4, and 9, and adjust according to your dog's weight. Mix well to combine. Refrigerate any leftovers in an airtight container for up to 3 days.

TURKEY, PEAS, AND OATMEAL

MAKES 4 SERVINGS FOR A 50-POUND DOG

1½ cups uncooked oatmeal

½ cup frozen or canned peas

2 pounds ground turkey

¼ cup (2 ounces) low-fat cottage cheese

¼ cup (2 ounces) chicken liver, chopped

¼ cup canned pure pumpkin

1 Prepare the oats as directed on the package. Set it aside to cool. You should have about 2 cups of cooked oatmeal.

2 Cook the frozen peas according to the package directions. Once they've cooled (or if using canned), puree them in a food processor. You should have about ¼ cup of pea puree.

TO MAKE ONE SERVING

1⅓ cups raw ground turkey

½ cup cooked oatmeal

1 tablespoon pureed peas

1 tablespoon cottage cheese

1 tablespoon chopped raw chicken liver

1 tablespoon canned pumpkin

In your dog's bowl, combine the turkey, oatmeal, peas, cottage cheese, chicken liver, and pumpkin. Refer to the feeding chart on pages 34–35, columns 2, 3, 4, 5, and 9, and adjust according to your dog's weight. Mix well to combine. Refrigerate any leftovers in an airtight container for up to 3 days.

TURKEY, RED QUINOA, AND ANCHOVIES

MAKES 4 SERVINGS FOR A 50-POUND DOG

1 cup uncooked red quinoa

¼ cup canned unseasoned artichoke hearts, drained and chopped

2 pounds ground turkey

¼ cup mashed banana

¼ cup (2 ounces) anchovies, drained and chopped

1   Prepare the quinoa as directed on the package. Set it aside to cool. You should have about 2 cups of cooked quinoa.

TO MAKE ONE SERVING

1⅓ cups raw ground turkey

½ cup cooked red quinoa

1 tablespoon chopped artichoke hearts

1 tablespoon mashed banana

1 tablespoon chopped anchovies

In your dog's bowl, combine the turkey, quinoa, artichoke hearts, banana, and anchovies. Refer to the feeding chart on pages 34–35, columns 2, 3, 4, and 9, and adjust according to your dog's weight. Mix well to combine. Refrigerate any leftovers in an airtight container for up to 3 days.

TURKEY, MASHED POTATOES, AND GREEN BEANS

MAKES 4 SERVINGS FOR A 50-POUND DOG

3 medium red potatoes, diced

⅓ cups fresh green beans, chopped

2 pounds ground turkey

¼ cup (2 ounces) chopped chicken gizzard

¼ cup flaxseed meal

1. In a medium pot, cover the potatoes with water and bring to a boil. Cook until the potatoes are soft when pierced with the tip of a knife. Drain them and mash well in the pot. You should have about 2 cups of mashed potatoes.

2. Puree the green beans in a food processor. You should have about ¼ cup of green bean puree.

TO MAKE ONE SERVING

1⅓ cups raw ground turkey

½ cup mashed potato

1 tablespoon pureed green beans

1 tablespoon raw chicken gizzard

1 tablespoon flaxseed meal

In your dog's bowl, combine the turkey, potato, green beans, gizzard, and flaxseed meal. Refer to the feeding chart on pages 34–35, columns 2, 3, 4, 5, and 9, and adjust according to your dog's weight. Mix well to combine. Refrigerate any leftovers in an airtight container for up to 3 days.

TURKEY, COUSCOUS, AND KALE

MAKES 4 SERVINGS FOR A 50-POUND DOG

1 cup uncooked couscous

½ cup chopped kale

2 pounds ground turkey

¼ cup plain yogurt

¼ cup (2 ounces) chopped beef heart

1   Prepare the couscous as directed on the package. Set it aside to cool. You should have about 2 cups of cooked couscous.

2   Fill a large saucepan with 1 inch of water and place a vegetable steamer inside the pan. Place the kale in the steamer. Bring the water to a boil and steam the kale until bright green and wilted. Remove the steamer basket. Place the kale in a bowl and set aside to cool. You should have about ¼ cup of steamed kale.

TO MAKE ONE SERVING

1⅓ cups raw ground turkey

½ cup cooked couscous

1 tablespoon steamed kale

1 tablespoon plain yogurt

1 tablespoon raw beef heart

In your dog's bowl, combine the turkey, couscous, kale, yogurt, and beef heart. Refer to the feeding chart on pages 34–35, columns 2, 3, 4, 5, and 9, and adjust according to your dog's weight. Mix well to combine. Refrigerate any leftovers in an airtight container for up to 3 days.

CHICKEN, BROWN RICE, AND CHICKPEAS

MAKES 4 SERVINGS FOR A 50-POUND DOG

¾ cup uncooked brown rice

¼ cup canned chickpeas

2 pounds ground chicken

¼ cup wheat germ

¼ cup (2 ounces) low-fat cottage cheese

1 Prepare the rice as directed on the package. Set it aside to cool. You should have about 2 cups of cooked rice.

2 Puree the chickpeas in a food processor with a little bit of the liquid from the can, if needed. You should have about ¼ cup of chickpea puree.

TO MAKE ONE SERVING

1⅓ cups raw ground chicken

½ cup cooked brown rice

1 tablespoon pureed chickpeas

1 tablespoon wheat germ

1 tablespoon cottage cheese

In your dog's bowl, combine the chicken, rice, chickpeas, wheat germ, and cottage cheese. Refer to the feeding chart on pages 34–35, columns 2, 3, 4, and 9, and adjust according to your dog's weight. Mix well to combine. Refrigerate any leftovers in an airtight container for up to 3 days.

CHICKEN, RED QUINOA, AND ASPARAGUS

MAKES 4 SERVINGS FOR A 50-POUND DOG

1 cup uncooked red quinoa

½ cup asparagus, chopped

2 pounds ground chicken

¼ cup (2 ounces) chopped chicken liver

¼ cup plain Greek yogurt

1 Prepare the quinoa as directed on the package. Set it aside to cool. You should have about 2 cups of cooked quinoa.

2 Puree the asparagus in a food processor. You should have about ¼ cup of asparagus puree.

TO MAKE ONE SERVING

1⅓ cups raw ground chicken

½ cup cooked red quinoa

1 tablespoon pureed asparagus

1 tablespoon plain Greek yogurt

1 tablespoon raw chicken liver

In your dog's bowl, combine the chicken, quinoa, asparagus, yogurt, and chicken liver. Refer to the feeding chart on pages 34–35, columns 2, 3, 4, 5, and 9, and adjust according to your dog's weight. Mix well to combine. Refrigerate any leftovers in an airtight container for up to 3 days.

CHICKEN, COUSCOUS, AND YELLOW SQUASH

MAKES 4 SERVINGS FOR A 50-POUND DOG

1 cup uncooked couscous

½ cup diced yellow squash

2 pounds ground chicken

¼ cup (2 ounces) chopped beef heart

¼ cup (2 ounces) canned sardines, drained

1 Prepare the couscous as directed on the package. Set it aside to cool. You should have about 2 cups of cooked couscous.

2 Pure the squash in a food processor and set it aside. You should have about ¼ cup of squash puree.

TO MAKE ONE SERVING

1⅓ cups raw ground chicken

½ cup cooked couscous

¼ cup pureed yellow squash

1 tablespoon sardines

1 tablespoon raw beef heart

In your dog's bowl, combine the chicken, couscous, squash, sardines, and beef heart. Refer to the feeding chart on pages 34–35, columns 2, 3, 4, 5, and 9, and adjust according to your dog's weight. Mix well to combine. Refrigerate any leftovers in an airtight container for up to 3 days.

CHICKEN PASTA

MAKES 4 SERVINGS FOR A 50-POUND DOG

1 cup uncooked quinoa pasta

1 small red beet

2 pounds ground chicken

¼ cup flaxseed meal

1 Prepare the pasta as directed on the package. Set it aside to cool. You should have about 2 cups of cooked pasta.

2 Place the beet in a small saucepan with enough water to cover. Bring the water to a boil and cook for about 45 minutes, or until the beet is tender. Set it aside to cool. Once cooled, peel the beet, dice it, then puree it in a food processor. You should have about ¼ cup of beet puree.

TO MAKE ONE SERVING

1⅓ cups raw ground chicken

½ cup cooked pasta

1 tablespoon pureed beet

1 tablespoon flaxseed meal

In your dog's bowl, combine the chicken, pasta, beets, and flaxseed meal. Refer to the feeding chart on pages 34–35, columns 2, 3, 4, and 9, and adjust according to your dog's weight. Mix well to combine. Refrigerate any leftovers in an airtight container for up to 3 days.

CHAPTER 4

TREAT RECIPES

A DOG'S DAY JUST WOULDN'T BE COMPLETE WITHOUT A TREAT OR TWO. For owners, treats are a great tool to use as reward and motivation for training and to reinforce good behavior. For dogs, they're a much-anticipated midmorning or midafternoon snack they come to expect. I've gotten into the habit of giving my dogs their first treat of the day after their morning walks, and once we round the corner to the house they all eagerly rush through the gate to take their seated positions on the deck. They also seem to know when it's 4 P.M. and time for treat number 2!

For all the treat recipes, I suggest using a spoon to measure out the balls of dough on the baking sheet. For my dogs, which are between 50 and 65 pounds, I use a tablespoon to measure out the dough but you can certainly vary the size of the cookies depending on your dog's size. I intentionally make the treats smaller so that I can put them in a toy to give them a challenging game with a tasty reward at the end. Because ovens and cooking times vary, especially if you're going to adjust the size of the cookies, always monitor the cookies while they're baking, and always allow them to cool completely before serving. I use a collander to cool them, placing them on one layer around the sides. Once they're cooled they should be soft in the middle and easy to break apart.

I use organ meat, which is very nutrient rich, in several of these recipes, so if you make those cookies be sure to moderate the organ meat you're giving in the main meal. Because organ meat is so rich an excessive amount of it can loosen your dog's stool and even cause diarrhea.

PUMPKIN SPICE TREATS
MAKES 4 DOZEN

When I make treats for my dogs I usually make them in large batches and freeze them. Since I have four dogs with different favorites, I usually dedicate a Sunday afternoon to making a few different types of cookies and stocking up for the upcoming weeks. In all of the recipes that call for organ meat, be sure to mince the beef heart into very small pieces, to distribute it evenly throughout the batter.

2 large eggs	½ cup (4 ounces) chopped beef heart
2½ cups whole wheat flour	½ cup hot water
1 cup (8 ounces) pumpkin	1 tablespoon cinnamon
1 cup mashed ripe banana	

1 Preheat the oven to 325°F. Coat a baking sheet with nonstick cooking spray or line it with parchment paper.

2 In a large bowl, beat the eggs. Add the flour, pumpkin, banana, beef heart, water, and cinnamon. Mix all the ingredients well.

3 Drop rounded tablespoons of dough onto the prepared baking sheet about ½ inch apart from each other. (Spray or line a second baking sheet if you run out of room on the first.) Bake them for 15–18 minutes, until slightly hardened. Allow the treats to cool for 30 minutes before serving. Refrigerate them in an airtight container for up to 3 days or freeze for up to 3 months.

CESAR'S FAVORITE CHICKEN LIVER TREATS

MAKES 5 DOZEN

When his owners first rescued Cesar, he was very underweight and malnourished. He also suffered from a very dry coat and skin and was constantly itching. For the first few months in his new home, Cesar's owners fed him dry dog food and he didn't seem to gain much weight. He also continued to itch, and was losing some of his fur from constant scratching. After a few months, his owner began making him homemade food. After several weeks he stopped itching completely and began to gain weight. I hear stories like this all the time and am always happy when owners move to a homemade diet, as it can drastically improve the health and well-being of a dog with nutritious, healthy ingredients like the chicken liver, eggs, and pumpkin in this recipe.

½ cup (4 ounces) chicken liver

2 large eggs

2 cups whole wheat flour

1 cup canned pure pumpkin

½ cup creamy peanut butter

½ cup hot water

¼ teaspoon ground cinnamon

1 Preheat the oven to 325°F. Coat a baking sheet with nonstick cooking spray or line it with parchment paper.

2 Using kitchen scissors, cut the chicken liver into bite-size pieces and set it aside in a small bowl.

3 In a large bowl, beat the eggs. Add the liver, flour, pumpkin, peanut butter, water, and cinnamon. Mix them together well.

4 Drop rounded tablespoons of dough onto the prepared baking sheet about ½ inch apart from each other. (Spray or line a second baking sheet if you run out of room on the first.) Bake them for 15–18 minutes, until slightly hardened. Allow the treats to cool for 30 minutes before serving. Refrigerate them in an airtight container for up to 3 days or freeze for up to 3 months.

PORK LOIN FRITTERS
MAKES 3 DOZEN

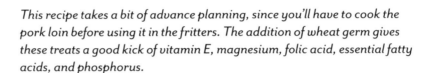

This recipe takes a bit of advance planning, since you'll have to cook the pork loin before using it in the fritters. The addition of wheat germ gives these treats a good kick of vitamin E, magnesium, folic acid, essential fatty acids, and phosphorus.

6 ounces pork loin

¼ cup uncooked grits

¼ cup (2 ounces) chicken liver

2 large eggs

2 cups whole wheat flour

½ cup wheat germ

½ cup hot water

1 Preheat the oven to 350°F. Coat a roasting pan with nonstick cooking spray.

2 Place the pork loin in the prepared pan and roast, uncovered, for about 20 minutes or until the internal temperature reaches 145°F. Remove the pork from the oven and set aside to cool.

3 Reduce the oven temperature to 325°F. Coat a baking sheet with nonstick cooking spray or line it with parchment paper.

4 Prepare the grits as directed on the package. Set them aside to cool. You should have about ½ cup of cooked grits.

5 Finely mince the cooled pork in a food processor. You should have about 1 cup of minced pork. Add the chicken liver to the processor and puree.

6 In a large bowl, beat the eggs. Add the grits, pork-liver mixture, flour, wheat germ, and water. Mix them together well.

7 Drop rounded tablespoons of dough onto the prepared baking sheet about ½ inch apart from each other. (Spray or line a second baking sheet if you run out of room on the first.) Bake them for 12 to 15 minutes, until slightly hardened. Allow the treats to cool for 30 minutes before serving. Refrigerate them in an airtight container for up to 3 days or freeze for up to 3 months.

SARDINE AND OATMEAL TARTS
MAKES 4 DOZEN

———— ⬡ ————

Rich in vitamin B and fiber, oats are healthy for dogs. I use quick-cooking oatmeal in most of my recipes but you can substitute rolled oats; they take a bit longer to cook and may change the texture of the cookies slightly. If you use canned sardines that come whole, be sure to chop them into small pieces before folding them into the batter.

2 large eggs

3 cups quick-cooking oatmeal

1 cup creamy peanut butter

½ cup (4 ounces) canned sardines, drained

½ cup hot water

1   Preheat the oven to 325°F. Coat a baking sheet with nonstick cooking spray or line it with parchment paper.

2   In a large bowl, beat the eggs. Add the oatmeal, peanut butter, sardines, and water. Mix them together well.

3   Drop rounded tablespoons of dough onto the prepared baking sheet about ½ inch apart from each other. (Spray or line a second baking sheet if you run out of room on the first.) Bake them for 15–18 minutes, until slightly hardened. Allow the treats to cool for 30 minutes before serving. Refrigerate them in an airtight container for up to 3 days or freeze for up to 3 months.

CHICKEN BISCUITS
MAKES 4 DOZEN

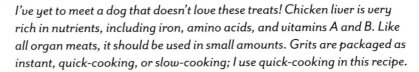

I've yet to meet a dog that doesn't love these treats! Chicken liver is very rich in nutrients, including iron, amino acids, and vitamins A and B. Like all organ meats, it should be used in small amounts. Grits are packaged as instant, quick-cooking, or slow-cooking; I use quick-cooking in this recipe.

1 cup quick-cooking grits

2 large eggs

2 cups whole wheat flour

¼ cup (2 ounces) chopped chicken liver

¼ cup wheat germ

¼ cup unsalted chicken broth

1   Preheat the oven to 325°F. Coat a baking sheet with nonstick cooking spray or line it with parchment paper.

2   Cook the grits according to the package directions. Set them aside to cool. You should have about 2 cups of cooked grits.

3   In a large bowl, beat the eggs. Add the cooled grits, flour, liver, wheat germ, and broth. Mix them together well.

4   Drop rounded tablespoons of dough onto the prepared baking sheet about ½ inch apart from each other. (Spray or line a second baking sheet if you run out of room on the first.) Bake for 15–18 minutes, until slightly hardened. Allow the treats to cool for 30 minutes before serving. Refrigerate them in an airtight container for up to 3 days or freeze for up to 3 months.

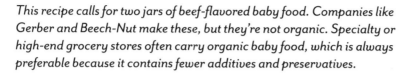

VEGGIE OATMEAL BITES

MAKES 4 DOZEN

This recipe calls for two jars of beef-flavored baby food. Companies like Gerber and Beech-Nut make these, but they're not organic. Specialty or high-end grocery stores often carry organic baby food, which is always preferable because it contains fewer additives and preservatives.

½ cup (4 ounces) chopped carrots

½ cup (4 ounces) peas

2 large eggs

3 cups uncooked quick-cooking oatmeal

2 (2.5-ounce) jars beef-flavored baby food

½ cup hot water

1 Preheat the oven to 325°F. Coat a baking sheet with nonstick cooking spray or line it with parchment paper.

2 Fill a small pot with water and bring to a boil. Add the carrots and boil until soft, about 20 minutes. Remove from the water, drain, and set aside to cool. Once cooled, puree in a food processor. Remove the carrot puree from the food processor and puree the peas.

3 In a large bowl, beat the eggs. Add the oatmeal, the pureed carrot, the pureed peas, the baby food, and the water. Mix them together well.

4 Drop rounded tablespoons of dough onto the prepared baking sheet about ½ inch apart from each other. (Spray or line a second baking sheet if you run out of room on the first.) Bake them for 15–18 minutes, until slightly hardened. Allow the treats to cool for 30 minutes before serving. Refrigerate them in an airtight container for up to 3 days or freeze for up to 3 months.

BANANA BREAKFAST BITES

MAKES 4 DOZEN

These nutritious bites are a healthy breakfast treat. The combination of ground beef and chicken broth make these treats a favorite among dogs who love meat, like mine. The puffed rice cereal adds a nice crunch while the banana adds fiber, potassium, vitamins A, B, E, C, and K, and folate.

3 cups puffed rice cereal

1¼ cups unsalted beef or chicken broth

1¼ cups whole wheat flour

1 cup thinly sliced banana

8 ounces ground beef

1 large egg

1   Preheat the oven to 350°F. Coat a baking sheet with nonstick cooking spray or line it with parchment paper.

2   In a large bowl, combine the cereal and broth and let them soak for 10 minutes, until the cereal has absorbed most of the broth.

3   Add the flour, banana, beef, and egg to the bowl and mix well.

4   Drop rounded tablespoons of dough onto the prepared baking sheet about ½ inch apart from each other. (Spray or line a second baking sheet if you run out of room on the first.) Bake them for 15–18 minutes, until slightly hardened. Allow the treats to cool for 30 minutes before serving. Refrigerate them in an airtight container for up to 3 days or freeze for up to 3 months.

PEANUT BUTTER AND COCONUT CAKES

MAKES 4 DOZEN

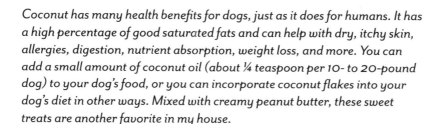

Coconut has many health benefits for dogs, just as it does for humans. It has a high percentage of good saturated fats and can help with dry, itchy skin, allergies, digestion, nutrient absorption, weight loss, and more. You can add a small amount of coconut oil (about ¼ teaspoon per 10- to 20-pound dog) to your dog's food, or you can incorporate coconut flakes into your dog's diet in other ways. Mixed with creamy peanut butter, these sweet treats are another favorite in my house.

4 cups unsweetened cornflakes	½ cup creamy peanut butter
1 cup unsweetened shredded coconut	½ cup hot water
1 cup whole wheat flour	2 large eggs

1 Preheat the oven to 325°F. Coat a baking sheet with nonstick cooking spray or line it with parchment paper.

2 In a large bowl, crush the cornflakes into crumbs by hand or with a potato masher. Add the coconut, flour, peanut butter, water, and eggs and mix well.

3 Drop rounded tablespoons of dough onto the prepared baking sheet about ½ inch apart from each other. (Spray or line a second baking sheet if you run out of room on the first.) Bake for 15–18 minutes, until slightly hardened. Allow the treats to cool for 30 minutes before serving. Refrigerate them in an airtight container for up to 3 days or freeze for up to 3 months.

PACO'S PEANUT BUTTER CUPS
MAKES 3 DOZEN

———— ⟨⊃□⊂⟩ ————

A homemade diet often cures a lot of allergy problems in dogs. Many dogs develop allergies simply because they are eating the same thing, day after day, year after year. Some dogs, however, have an allergy to a specific ingredient. While I was writing this book, I met Paco—a Westie—who is allergic to beef and chicken. This simple treat recipe, along with Chuleta's Chickpea Fritters (page 125), was created for him and other dogs who are allergic to cereal grains, beef, or chicken.

2 large eggs

2 cups quick-cooking oats

1 cup shredded part-skim mozzarella cheese

½ cup creamy peanut butter

¼ cup hot water

1 Preheat the oven to 325°F. Coat a baking sheet with nonstick cooking spray or line it with parchment paper.

2 In a large bowl, beat the eggs. Add the oats, mozzarella, peanut butter, and water and mix well.

3 Drop rounded tablespoons of dough onto the prepared baking sheet about ½ inch apart from each other. (Spray or line a second baking sheet if you run out of room on the first.) Bake them for 15–18 minutes, until slightly hardened. Allow the treats to cool on the baking sheet for 30 minutes before serving. Refrigerate them in an airtight container for up to 3 days or freeze for up to 3 months.

CHULETA'S CHICKPEA FRITTERS

MAKES 4 TO 5 DOZEN

Chuleta ("Porkchop" in Spanish) was adopted from the Friends of Homeless Animals rescue organization in January 2010. Although her first few years prior to being rescued weren't the happiest, she quickly settled into her new home and found the love she deserves. These days, her time is spent frolicking with her dog pals and hogging the couch (she may be small, but those legs can really sprawl), always making time to exchange a few high-fives for her one of favorite homemade treats!

2 large eggs

2½ cups chickpea flour

2 (5-ounce) cans solid white tuna in water, drained

½ cup creamy peanut butter

½ cup hot water

1. Preheat the oven to 325°F. Coat a baking sheet with nonstick cooking spray or line it with parchment paper.

2. In a large bowl, beat the eggs. Add the flour, tuna, peanut butter, and water and mix well.

3. Drop rounded tablespoons of dough onto the prepared baking sheet about ½ inch apart from each other. (Spray or line a second baking sheet if you run out of room on the first.) Bake them for 15–18 minutes, until slightly hardened. Allow the treats to cool for 30 minutes before serving. Refrigerate them in an airtight container for up to 3 days or freeze for up to 3 months.

CAMPER'S CAMPFIRE TREATS
MAKES 4 DOZEN

Camper was rescued in November of 2011 when he was only seventeen weeks old. Camper's cute all-black face and serious eyes caught his owners' attention, along with his calm demeanor and serious love of snuggling! It was only after they took him home that they discovered Camper's favorite pastime: running. Although some of his favorite treats are carrots, pickles, and apples, Camper never turns down these delicious turkey bacon treats, which really help fuel all his laps around the dog park.

8 ounces turkey bacon	¼ cup hot water
2 cups whole wheat flour	2 large eggs
½ cup unsalted beef broth	

1. Preheat the oven to 350°F. Coat a baking sheet with nonstick cooking spray or line it with parchment paper.

2. Place the uncooked bacon in a food processor and pulse to roughly chop it. Transfer it to a large bowl. Add the flour, broth, water, and eggs and mix well.

3. Drop rounded tablespoons of dough onto the prepared baking sheet about ½ inch apart from each other. (Spray or line a second baking sheet if you run out of room on the first.) Bake them for 15–18 minutes, until slightly hardened. Allow the treats to cool for 30 minutes before serving. Refrigerate them in an airtight container for up to 3 days or freeze for up to 3 months.

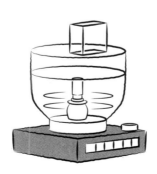

BELLA'S BEEF BITES

MAKES 4 DOZEN

Bella is a seven-year-old Golden Retriever who loves to go on long walks, but a few years ago she tore her ACL while jumping off a dune at the beach. While she recovered from surgery to repair her knee, her owner put her on a homemade diet to help control her weight while her exercise was limited. Certain breeds tend to gain weight more easily than others, and Golden Retrievers fall into this category. Homemade diets are beneficial for dogs with weight problems because the ingredients are fresher and contain fewer additives, preservatives, and unnecessary fats, making weight control easier.

2 large eggs

2½ cups amaranth flour

8 ounces ground beef

½ cup hot water

½ cup carob powder

1 Preheat the oven to 350°F. Coat a baking sheet with nonstick cooking spray or line it with parchment paper.

2 In a small bowl, combine the carob powder and the hot water and stir until smooth.

3 In a large bowl, beat the eggs. Add the flour, beef, water, and carob mixture and mix well.

4 Drop rounded tablespoons of dough onto the prepared baking sheet about ½ inch apart from each other. (Spray or line a second baking sheet if you run out of room on the first.) Bake them for 15–18 minutes, until slightly hardened. Allow the treats to cool for 30 minutes before serving. Refrigerate them in an airtight container for up to 3 days or freeze for up to 3 months.

SWEET POTATO DUMPLINGS
MAKES 4 DOZEN

Sweet potatoes are another staple in my house. My dogs love them, they're inexpensive, and they're super-healthy. The natural sweetness of the potato combined with the rich, sweet flavor of the chickpea flour makes these treats a front-runner!

1 small sweet potato	½ cup hot water
2½ cups chickpea flour	2 large eggs
½ pound (8 ounces) raw ground chicken	

1. Preheat the oven to 325°F. Coat a baking sheet with nonstick cooking spray or line it with parchment paper.

2. In a medium pot, cover the sweet potato with water and bring it to a boil. Cook it until it is soft when pierced with the tip of a knife. Drain it and mash well in the pot. Set it aside to cool for 10 minutes. You should have about 1 cup of mashed sweet potato.

3. Add the flour, chicken, water, and eggs to the mashed sweet potato and mix well.

4. Drop rounded tablespoons of dough onto the prepared baking sheet about ½ inch apart from each other. (Spray or line a second baking sheet if you run out of room on the first.) Bake them for 15–18 minutes, until slightly hardened. Allow the treats to cool for 30 minutes before serving. Refrigerate them in an airtight container for up to 3 days or freeze for up to 3 months.

TURKEY BACON TREATS
MAKES 4 DOZEN

On Sunday mornings when I'm making brunch, I can always count on my pack to be right behind me in the kitchen when it's time to fry the turkey bacon. It has an aroma no dog can resist! These treats combine turkey bacon with amaranth flour, which is a sweet, gluten-free flour that adds nice flavor. I can usually find amaranth flour in a specialty grocery store, but if you can't find it, you can always substitute regular or whole wheat flour.

8 ounces turkey bacon	½ cup hot water
2 cups amaranth flour	2 large eggs

1 Preheat the oven to 350°F. Coat a baking sheet with nonstick cooking spray or line it with parchment paper.

2 Place the uncooked bacon in a food processor and roughly chop it. Transfer it to a large bowl. Add the flour, water, and eggs and mix well.

3 Drop rounded tablespoons of dough onto the prepared baking sheet about ½ inch apart from each other. (Spray or line a second baking sheet if you run out of room on the first.) Bake them for 15–18 minutes, until slightly hardened. Allow the treats to cool for 30 minutes before serving. Refrigerate them in an airtight container for up to 3 days or freeze for up to 3 months.

THANKSGIVING BITES
MAKES 3 DOZEN

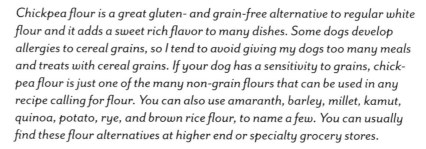

Chickpea flour is a great gluten- and grain-free alternative to regular white flour and it adds a sweet rich flavor to many dishes. Some dogs develop allergies to cereal grains, so I tend to avoid giving my dogs too many meals and treats with cereal grains. If your dog has a sensitivity to grains, chickpea flour is just one of the many non-grain flours that can be used in any recipe calling for flour. You can also use amaranth, barley, millet, kamut, quinoa, potato, rye, and brown rice flour, to name a few. You can usually find these flour alternatives at higher end or specialty grocery stores.

2½ cups chickpea flour	½ cup wheat germ
8 ounces raw ground turkey	¼ cup hot water
½ cup canned pure pumpkin	2 large eggs

1 Preheat the oven to 325°F. Coat a baking sheet with nonstick cooking spray or line it with parchment paper.

2 In a large bowl, mix all the ingredients together.

3 Drop rounded tablespoons of dough on the prepared baking sheet about ½ inch apart from each other. (Spray or line a second baking sheet if you run out of room on the first.) Bake them for 15-18 minutes, until slightly hardened. Allow the treats to cool on the baking sheet for 30 minutes before serving. Store them in an airtight container in the refrigerator for up to 3 days or freeze for up to 3 months.

CHAPTER 5

SPECIAL
OCCASION RECIPES

FOR THOSE SPECIAL OCCASIONS WHEN STANDARD TREATS JUST AREN'T SPECIAL ENOUGH, here are some delicious and nutritious recipes for celebrating birthdays and holidays. I've also included two quick-and-easy no-bake recipes great for on-the-go meals and travel, as well as two recipes for homemade KONG pastes. KONGs are my secret weapon in keeping my four-dog household cool, calm, and collected!

For these recipes, you'll want to have a baking sheet, parchment paper, nonstick cooking spray, and a 12-cup muffin tin on hand, as well as your trusty food processor if you're making the KONG pastes. For the cookie recipes, I use a regular spoon to measure the dough but you may want to vary the cookie sizes depending on the size of your dog.

Always keep an eye on the cookies and muffins as they're baking, as cooking times and ovens may vary slightly. Always allow them to cool completely before feeding them to your dog. When it comes to serving sizes, use your judgment based on the size and activity level of your dog. Since these recipes are intended for special occasions, you can simply give your dog a serving or two of these treats in place of treats you would normally give him for that day so you do not overfeed.

KONG PASTES

KONGs are great toys to have on hand, especially if you have multiple dogs like I do. KONGs are essentially rubber balls with a hole in the center where you can put treats or pastes. I've seen the pastes sold at pet stores for upward of $8 a tube, so I decided to whip up my own recipes, which are much healthier and cheaper. In addition to these pastes, you can get creative and use your dog's favorite treats in the KONGs and enjoy some peace and quiet while they work on getting them out! I usually pack KONGs with these pastes—or peanut butter if I'm short on time—and freeze them for occasions when I have to go out for a longer period of time. They are a great toy for combatting separation anxiety and satisfying chewing urges.

PORK LOIN PÂTÉ

MAKES 1 CUP

—— ⟨⎯⟩ ——

1 cup chopped cooked pork loin (about 6 ounces raw; see page 46 for cooking instructions)

¼ cup (2 ounces) anchovies, drained and chopped

2 tablespoons light coconut milk

1 Pulse all ingredients in a food processor until they form a thick paste.

2 Using a tablespoon or teaspoon (depending on the size of the KONG), fill the center with enough paste to coat the inside. Freeze it for 1 hour, then serve. Refrigerate the leftover paste in an airtight container for up to 3 days.

CHICKEN AND CHEESE PÂTÉ

MAKES 1 CUP

—— ⟨⎯⟩ ——

4 ounces boneless chicken breast

2 tablespoons unsalted butter

½ cup (4½ ounces) chicken liver

2 tablespoons cream cheese

1 Place the chicken breasts in a large pot with enough water to cover completely. Bring the water to a boil, then reduce the heat to medium-high and cook for 15 to 20 minutes, until the chicken is no longer pink in the middle. Set aside to cool. Chop the cooled chicken into bite-size pieces. You should have about ½ cup of chopped chicken.

2 In a small saucepan over medium-low heat, melt the butter. Add the liver and sauté for 2 to 3 minutes, until slightly browned. Add the chicken and sauté it for 1 minute. Pour the mixture into a food processor. Add the cream cheese and process until pureed.

3 Using a tablespoon or teaspoon (depending on the size of the KONG), fill the center with enough paste to coat the inside. Freeze it for 1 hour, then serve. Refrigerate the leftover paste in an airtight container for up to 3 days or freeze for up to 3 months.

These no-bake recipes are great in a pinch or if you don't have access to a stove. I also make these if I'm traveling with my dogs, as both can be prepared ahead of time, packed in a sandwich bag, and stored in a cooler. (If I am taking them on the go, I pack them as sandwiches and break them up in my dogs' bowls before feeding.) I keep a good stock of tuna and chicken salad cans so I have a backup if I don't have time to cook or if my power goes out. I also stock up on different Ezekiel-brand breads, delicious high-fiber sprouted-grain breads, which are easy to freeze and are a good go-to for these quick recipes. You can also use other types of gluten-free and whole-grain breads as a substitution.

CHICKEN SALAD SANDWICH
MAKES 1 SERVING FOR A 50-POUND DOG

2 slices Ezekiel sprouted-grain bread
1 (8-ounce) can chicken, drained
1 tablespoon chopped celery

In your dog's bowl, break the slices of bread into small pieces. Mix in the chicken and celery and serve. Refrigerate any leftovers in an airtight container for up to 3 days.

TUNA AND CHEESE WRAP
MAKES 1 SERVING FOR A 50-POUND DOG

1 Ezekiel sprouted whole-grain tortilla
1 (8-ounce) can solid white tuna in water, drained
1 tablespoon shredded part-skim cheese

In your dog's bowl, break the tortilla into small pieces. Add in the tuna and the cheese and serve. Refrigerate any leftovers in an airtight container for up to 3 days.

CARROT CAKE
MAKES 1 (8-BY-8-INCH) CAKE

2 cups chopped carrots

2 large eggs

2 cups whole wheat flour

1 cup (8 ounces) canned sardines,
drained

½ cup sunflower seed oil

½ cup warm water

2 cups low-fat cream cheese

1   Preheat the oven to 350°F. Coat an 8-by-8-inch baking pan with nonstick cooking spray.

2   Puree the carrots in a food processor. You should have about 2 cups of carrot puree.

3   In a large bowl, beat the eggs. Add the carrot puree, flour, sardines, oil, and water and mix well.

4   Pour the batter into the prepared pan and distribute it evenly. Bake it for 35 minutes, until golden brown on top. Allow the cake to cool completely in the pan, about 30 minutes, before serving. Once the cake is cooled, ice the top with the cream cheese. Cut pieces about 2 inches square, then break up a piece in your dog's bowl and serve. Cover the leftovers with foil and refrigerate for up to 3 days or freeze for up to 3 months.

SUNFLOWER AND COCONUT CUPCAKES

MAKES 12 CUPCAKES

These "pup" cakes have a surprise in the middle your dog will probably be delighted to discover: a dollop of fresh ground beef! It may sound unappealing to you, but my dogs go nuts for these and hopefully yours will too. The sunflower oil and coconut give these cupcakes a delicious taste and a boost of vitamins, omega-3s, and immune defense. Coconut also has many antibacterial effects, which makes it good for your dog too.

7 medium red potatoes, diced

2 large eggs

¼ cup sunflower seed oil

¾ pound (12 ounces) ground beef

1 cup unsweetened shredded coconut

1　Preheat the oven to 375°F. Line a 12-cup muffin tin with paper liners and coat each one with nonstick cooking spray.

2　Place the potatoes in a large saucepan with enough water to cover. Bring the water to a boil and cook them until they are soft when pierced with the tip of a knife, about 25 minutes. Drain them and mash well in the pan. You should have about 5 cups of mashed potatoes.

3　In a large bowl, beat the eggs. Add the mashed potatoes and the oil and mix well.

4　Fill each muffin cup halfway with the batter. Place 1 tablespoon of the beef in the middle of each cupcake. Fill the cups with batter, almost to the top. Top each cupcake with about 1 tablespoon of the coconut.

5　Bake the cupcakes for 40 minutes until golden brown on top. Allow the cupcakes to cool for 30 minutes in the pan before serving. Cover the leftovers with foil and refrigerate them for up to 3 days or freeze for up to 3 months.

RUBY'S RED VELVET CAKE
MAKES 1 (8-BY-8-INCH) CAKE

Ruby is a pit bull who was abandoned at a local shelter in 2010 after being used as a bait dog in a dog-fighting ring. She had just given birth to a litter of eleven adorable puppies, all of whom had been adopted out. Luckily for Ruby, one of the volunteers couldn't stand to see her at the shelter anymore and took Ruby home, where she now enjoys going for long walks, playing tug of war, and sleeping in!

3 medium red beets

½ cup carob powder

½ cup hot water

2 cups whole wheat flour

½ cup sunflower seed oil

2 large eggs

1 5-ounce can of tuna in water, drained

2 cups low-fat Greek yogurt

1   Preheat the oven to 350°F. Coat an 8-by-8-inch baking pan with non-stick cooking spray.

2   Place the beets in a small saucepan with enough water to cover. Bring the water to a boil and cook for about 45 minutes, or until the beets are tender. Set aside to cool. Once cooled, peel then dice the beets. Puree the diced beets in a food processor. Set aside. You should have about 2 cups of beet puree.

3   In a large bowl, combine the carob powder and hot water and stir until smooth. Add the beet puree, flour, oil, tuna, and eggs and mix well.

4   Pour the batter into the prepared pan and distribute it evenly. Bake it for 40 minutes, until golden brown on top. Allow the cake to cool completely in the pan, about 30 minutes, before serving. Once the cake is cooled, ice the top with the yogurt. Cut pieces about 2 inches square, then break up a piece in your dog's bowl and serve. Cover the leftovers with foil and refrigerate for up to 3 days or freeze for up to 3 months.

MINI RICOTTA AND SARDINE CAKES

MAKES 12 CUPCAKES

1 (16.5-ounce) package yellow cake mix

Vegetable oil, as needed

Large eggs, as needed

½ cup (4 ounces) canned sardines, drained

¾ cup low-fat ricotta

1 Preheat the oven to 400°F. Line a 12-cup muffin tin with paper liners and coat each one with nonstick cooking spray.

2 Prepare the cake batter according to the package directions. Add the sardines to the batter and mix well.

3 Pour the batter into each muffin cup, filling them almost to the top. Bake the cupcakes for 15 to 18 minutes, until golden brown on top. Allow the cupcakes to cool for about 30 minutes in the pan before serving. Once cooled, top each cupcake with 1 tablespoon of the ricotta. Cover the leftovers with foil and refrigerate them for up to 3 days or freeze up to 3 months.

VALENTINE'S DAY COOKIES
MAKES 5 DOZEN

2 cups unsweetened cornflakes

2 cups whole wheat flour

1½ cups shredded low-fat mozzarella cheese

1½ cups (9 ounces) canned sardines, drained

½ cup hot water

¼ cup sunflower seed oil

2 large eggs

Red Cake Mate sugar crystals or red sprinkles

1 Preheat the oven to 325°F. Coat a baking sheet with nonstick cooking spray or line it with parchment paper.

2 In a large bowl, mash the cornflakes into crumbs by hand or with a potato masher. Add the flour, cheese, sardines, water, oil, and eggs and mix well.

3 Drop rounded tablespoons of dough onto the prepared baking sheet about ½ inch apart from each other. (Spray another baking sheet with nonstick cooking spray if you run out of room on the first.) Sprinkle 1 teaspoon of the sugar crystals on each cookie. Bake them for 12–15 minutes, until golden brown on top. Allow the cookies to cool for 30 minutes before serving. Refrigerate them in an airtight container for up to 3 days or freeze for up to 3 months.

TURKEY BACON AND OATMEAL CHRISTMAS COOKIES

MAKES 5 DOZEN

8 ounces turkey bacon

¼ cup carob powder

1 cup hot water

2 large eggs

2 cups oatmeal

1 ½ cups whole wheat flour

¼ cup sunflower seed oil

½ cup (4 ounces) chopped beef heart

Red Cake Mate sugar crystals or red sprinkles

1 Preheat the oven to 325°F. Coat a baking sheet with nonstick cooking spray or line it with parchment paper.

2 Place the uncooked turkey bacon in a food processor and pulse to roughly chop it.

3 In a small bowl, mix the carob powder and ½ cup of hot water to create a smooth paste.

4 In a large bowl, beat the eggs. Add the oatmeal, flour, oil, turkey bacon, beef heart, and the remaining ½ cup hot water. Add the carob powder paste and mix well.

5 Drop rounded tablespoons of dough onto the prepared baking sheet about ½ inch apart from each other. (Spray another baking sheet with nonstick cooking spray if you run out of room on the first.) Sprinkle 1 teaspoon of the sugar crystals on each cookie. Bake them for 12–15 minutes, until golden brown on top. Allow the cookies to cool for 30 minutes before serving. Refrigerate them in an airtight container for up to 3 days or freeze for up to 3 months.

PORK LOIN AND PUMPKIN MUFFINS

MAKES 12 MUFFINS

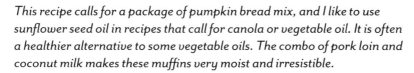

This recipe calls for a package of pumpkin bread mix, and I like to use sunflower seed oil in recipes that call for canola or vegetable oil. It is often a healthier alternative to some vegetable oils. The combo of pork loin and coconut milk makes these muffins very moist and irresistible.

1 pound pork loin

½ cup light coconut milk

1 (17.5-ounce) package pumpkin bread mix

Sunflower seed or vegetable oil, as needed

Eggs, as needed

¾ cup cream cheese, at room temperature

1. Preheat the oven to 400°F. Line a 12-cup muffin tin with paper liners and coat each one with nonstick cooking spray.

2. Finely chop the pork in a food processor and place it in a medium bowl. Add the coconut milk and refrigerate, covered, for 20 minutes to absorb.

3. Prepare the pumpkin bread batter according to package directions. Add the pork and coconut milk and mix well.

4. Fill each muffin cup almost to the top with batter. Bake the muffins for 25–30 minutes, until golden brown on top. Let the muffins cool for 30 minutes before serving. Once cooled, ice each muffin with 1 tablespoon of the cream cheese. Cover the leftovers with foil and refrigerate them for up to 3 days or freeze for up to 3 months.

BACON AND CREAM CHEESE MUFFINS

MAKES 12 MUFFINS

8 ounces turkey bacon

2 cups whole wheat flour

1 tablespoon baking powder

1 cup light coconut milk

¼ cup sunflower seed oil

2 large eggs, beaten

¾ cup cream cheese, at room temperature

1 Preheat the oven to 400°F. Line a 12-cup muffin tin with paper liners and coat each one with nonstick cooking spray.

2 Place the turkey bacon in a food processor and pulse to roughly chop it.

3 In a large bowl combine the flour and baking powder and mix well. Add the bacon, coconut milk, oil, and eggs and mix well.

4 Fill each muffin cup almost to the top with batter. Bake them for 25–30 minutes, until golden brown on top. Allow the muffins to cool for 30 minutes before serving. Once cooled, ice each muffin with 1 tablespoon of the cream cheese. Cover the leftovers with foil and refrigerate them for up to 3 days or freeze for up to 3 months.

ACKNOWLEDGMENTS

MY DOGS have brought into my life some of the most wonderful people I could have ever asked to bless my time on this miraculous planet Earth. In a specific way these individuals have helped me along my journey, which has been very much a path less traveled. An early morning walk on the beach with my dogs brought J.R. into my life. A simple question uttered from a complete stranger that morning changed the trajectory of my life and set me on course for what would be part of my ultimate calling.

I am beyond grateful that my editor and friend, Jackie Bondanza, saw something in me that I never saw in myself. We met while we were both volunteering for a local animal shelter; the idea for this project was her vision and I honestly did not believe I had the ability to write a book and bring it to fruition. I was very hesitant when she initially asked me to do a book but I was even more terrified of saying no. It has been a long labor and delivery, but Jackie has patiently endured my fits, tantrums, and mood swings when I simply could not spend one more minute in my kitchen. I am extremely grateful for her encouragement, support, and enthusiasm throughout this entire process.

Susan Radin deserves a special thank-you for the beautiful photos she shot for this book. Susan is a busy mom, wife, and dance educator, and I especially appreciate the countless hours she spent on this project. Her talent and creativity have been a huge inspiration in my life.

I must also express my love and gratitude for Jane Burke. Thank you for sharing your gifts and your healing hands. They have helped me grow into the Am that I am.

To Dr. Wayne Geltman and all the staff at All Creatures Veterinary Hospital, thank you for always being so kind and caring in taking care of our animals. Most importantly, I appreciate all the time Dr. Geltman has spent in contributing his expertise to this book.

My biggest supporter is my sister, Stephanie Filardi. Thank you for seeing the joy and the humor in my life. Words cannot express the gratitude I have for you—you are one of the few people who understand my soul. I love you.

To the animals that bless my life every day with love: thank you for making me laugh, and reminding me to take a nap and of the importance of playing nice.

Finally I must thank God. With him all things are possible. I thank God for having a better plan for my life than I ever could have imagined!

CONVERSION CHARTS

WEIGHT EQUIVALENTS

The metric weights given in this chart are not exact equivalents, but have been rounded up or down slightly to make measuring easier.

Avoirdupois	Metric
¼ ounce	7 grams
½ ounce	15 grams
1 ounce	30 grams
2 ounces	60 grams
3 ounces	90 grams
4 ounces	115 grams
5 ounces	150 grams
6 ounces	175 grams
7 ounces	200 grams
8 ounces (½ pound)	225 grams
9 ounces	250 grams
10 ounces	300 grams
11 ounces	325 grams
12 ounces	350 grams
13 ounces	375 grams
14 ounces	400 grams
15 ounces	425 grams
16 ounces (1 pound)	450 grams
1½ pounds	750 grams
2 pounds	900 grams
2¼ pounds	1 kilogram
3 pounds	1.4 kilograms
4 pounds	1.8 kilograms

VOLUME EQUIVALENTS

These are not exact equivalents for American cups and spoons, but have been rounded up or down slightly to make measuring easier.

American	Metric	Imperial
¼ teaspoon	1.2 milliliters	—
½ teaspoon	2.5 milliliters	—
1 teaspoon	5.0 milliliters	—
½ tablespoon (1½ teaspoons)	7.5 milliliters	—
1 tablespoon (3 teaspoons)	15 milliliters	—
¼ cup (4 tablespoons)	60 milliliters	2 fluid ounces
⅓ cup (5 tablespoons)	75 milliliters	2 ½ fluid ounces
½ cup (8 tablespoons)	125 milliliters	4 fluid ounces
⅔ cup (10 tablespoons)	150 milliliters	5 fluid ounces
¾ cup (12 tablespoons)	175 milliliters	6 fluid ounces
1 cup (16 tablespoons)	250 milliliters	8 fluid ounces
1¼ cups	300 milliliters	10 fluid ounces (½ pint)
1½ cups	350 milliliters	12 fluid ounces
2 cups (1 pint)	500 milliliters	16 fluid ounces
2½ cups	625 milliliters	20 fluid ounces (1 pint)
1 quart	1 liter	32 fluid ounces

OVEN TEMPERATURE EQUIVALENTS

Oven Mark	°F	°C	Gas
very cool	250–275	130–140	½–1
cool	300	150	2
warm	325	170	3
moderate	350	180	4
moderately hot	375–400	190–200	5–6
hot	425–450	220–230	7–8
very hot	475	250	9

INDEX

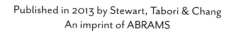

Published in 2013 by Stewart, Tabori & Chang
An imprint of ABRAMS

Library of Congress Control Number: 2013935970

ISBN: 978-1-61769-055-6

Editor: Jackie Bondanza
Designer: Alissa Faden
Production Manager: True Sims

The text of this book was composed in Mr Eaves and Populaire.

Printed and bound in USA

10 9 8 7 6 5 4 3

Stewart, Tabori & Chang books are available at special discounts when purchased in quantity for
premiums and promotions as well as fundraising or educational use. Special editions can also be
created to specification. For details, contact specialsales@abramsbooks.com or the address below.

ABRAMS
THE ART OF BOOKS SINCE 1949
115 West 18th Street
New York, NY 10011
www.abramsbooks.com